Mill

Rose
Lane

East

ROOKERY

ROMFORD

Warren Farm

Pudnal F.

Pigtail Farm

Lowlands

58

11

three
ills

Whalebone
House

10

Station

Whalebone

Pond

T.G.

Union house

Caphall

HAVERI

Crowlands

Fidlers hall

43

Rush G

Bell
house

Beacon tree

Heath

Lane

Mill

Valence

Eastbrook end

Eastbr
House

Tanyard

Valence
Wood

Five Elms

Myalls

raltar

Plan of Romford in the mid-19th century. Little development has taken place, but the Eastern Counties Railway have at least built their railway station near to the centre of the town.

ROMFORD

A History

Brian Evans

Looking east along the Market, late 1930s

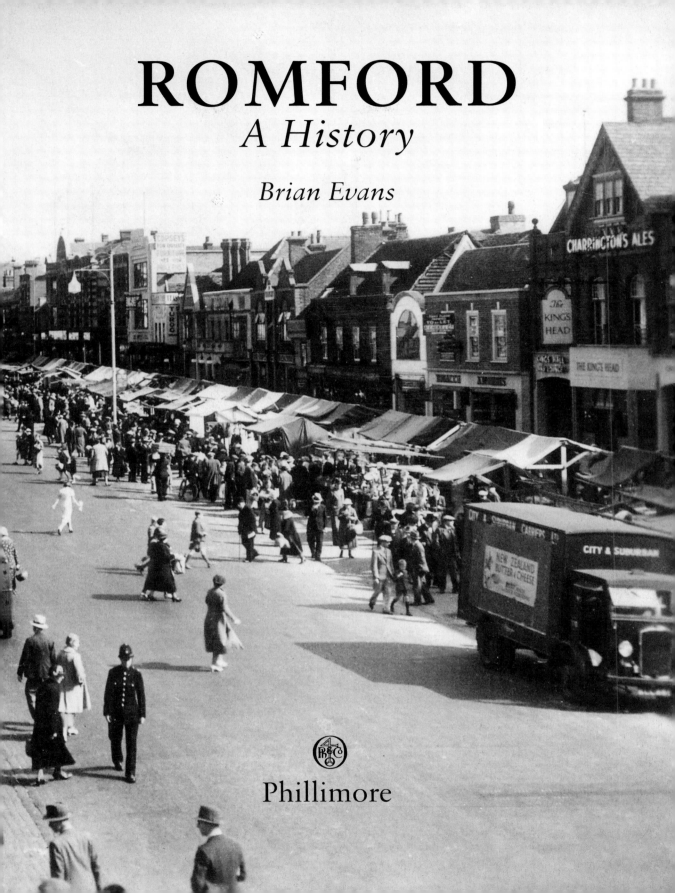

ROMFORD
A History

Brian Evans

Phillimore

2006

Published by
PHILLIMORE & CO. LTD
Shopwyke Manor Barn, Chichester, West Sussex, England
www.phillimore.co.uk

ISBN 1-86077-357 5
ISBN 13 978-1-86077-357 0

Printed and bound in Great Britain by
CROMWELL PRESS LTD
Trowbridge, Wiltshire

CONTENTS

List of Illustrations   vii
Acknowledgements   ix
Introduction   xi

1 *Origins*   1
2 *Putting Romford on the Map*   9
3 *Kings, Queens and Citizens of the Liberty*   15
4 *Fashionable Times*   29
5 *Eventful Century*   41
6 *In the Line of Duty*   65
7 *The Golden Mile and Civic Pride*   71
8 *War Comes Home*   89
9 *New Prosperity*   101

Bibliography   111
Index   113

Dedication

To the incomparable Susan

LIST OF ILLUSTRATIONS

Frontispiece: The Market, late 1930s

1 Marks Manor at edge of forest, 1662	1	41 Gidea Hall, *c*.1908 — 33
2 Lowlands in London Road, 1900	2	42 Act of William III highway reparations — 34
3 Ancient dugout canoe	3	43 An early postboy — 34
4 An early Briton using a coracle	3	44 St Edward's Church, *c*.1840 — 35
5 An early drawing of the stones of Callanish	4	45 *The Cock and Bell Inn* — 35
6 Silver coin of the Iceni of East Anglia	4	46 William Smithfield, clockmaker — 36
7 Havering's connection to other megaliths	5	47 Queen Charlotte — 36
8 Roman milestone	6	48 The Whalebone toll-gate location — 37
9 Roman pavement stone	6	49 Romford toll-gate, mid-19th-century — 37
10 Hare Street, 1880	7	50 A house in North Street, Romford — 38
11 Stickleback Bridge, 1900s	7	51 Building opposite the 1787 Workhouse — 39
12 Saxon drinking horns	8	52 The Round House — 40
13 Edward the Confessor	8	53 Outside Repton's cottage at Hare Street — 42
14 Bow Bridge	10	54 Repton garden extension — 42
15 The estate map of Stewards Manor	12	55 The Royal Mail coach about 1820 — 43
16 Shields in Westminster Abbey choir aisles	13	56 Shops near the old St Edward's Church — 44
17 Seal of Simon de Montfort	14	57 Water pump in Main Road, Gidea Park — 44
18 The Havering halfpenny	15	58 Carrier wagon — 45
19 Old framework in the *Golden Lion* pub	16	59 The *Rising Sun* public house — 46
20 The Palace on the Havering Liberty map	17	60 The railway factory at Squirrels Heath — 47
21 Havering Chapel in 1818	18	61 Signalling by the railway police — 48
22 Old Liberty of Havering symbol	18	62 Hoy's donkey racing the train — 48
23 Plan of the former Palace	19	63 Advertisement for the railway extension — 49
24 Elizabeth I	20	64 The buildings of the 1838 Workhouse — 50
25 The Retreat	21	65 Romford Union governors — 50
26 The will of John Herde of Collier Row	22	66 Cartoon by 'Jack B.' — 51
27 Old courtyard east of Gidea Hall	22	67 Romford Cricket Club members — 51
28 Rear view of an Elizabethan house	23	68 Poster of cricket match — 52
29 *The Swan*	24	69 A busy cattle market — 52
30 Portrait of Francis Quarles	25	70 A plan of Market Place, Romford — 53
31 Stewards Manor from 1696 estate plan	25	71 Old High Street, Romford — 54
32 Marie de Medici leaves Gidea Hall	26	72 The submerged railway line — 55
33 A view of Marks Manor	27	73 The brewery after the flood — 56
34 The old *White Hart*	28	74 J.W. Lasham's business — 58
35 Token for the *Sun Inn*	29	75 New copper at Ind Coope's brewery — 59
36 Bowling along the road in a stage-coach	30	76 The opening of Romford Garden Suburb — 60
37 Carrier's cart	30	77 John Burns MP — 60
38 Old houses on the High Street, Romford	31	78 A corner of Meadway — 61
39 Strip plan of the turnpike road	32	79 Unique architect-designed houses — 61
40 View of Gidea Hall	33	80 A traffic-free South Street, *c*.1911 — 62

 81 A motor cab at Romford Station   62
 82 Motor vehicles in the High Street, *c*.1921   63
 83 An Ind Coope brewery motor vehicle   64
 84 Hare Street district   65
 85 Hare Hall camp   66
 86 Soldier posing with his lady   66
 87 Camp friendships   66
 88 Well-built huts   67
 89 Local ladies' soccer team   67
 90 Officers by the steps of Gidea Hall   68
 91 An autograph book sketch   68
 92 Soldiers, nurses, helpers and officers   69
 93 Drumhead service by the War Memorial   69
 94 The War Memorial   70
 95 Oliver and Ethel Fawkes   71
 96 London General buses in the Market Place   72
 97 Wireless advertising in the 1930s   72
 98 Panorama of South Street   73
 99 The Havana Cinema block   74
100 A view from the railway bridge, *c*.1905   75
101 Block of shops, 1954   75
102 H.W. Hole's advert, 1938   76
103 The next range of buildings northwards   76
104 Before South Street became less residential   77
105 Craddocks shop   77
106 Congregational Church to Sainsbury's   78
107 Two postmen with sacks of mail   78
108 Looking up from Western Road corner   79
109 South Street   80
110 An Edwardian scene in South Street   80
111 Top end of the panorama   81
112 Exchange Street   81
113 Wartime devastation   82
114 Quadrant Arcade elevation, 1954   83

115 West side of South Street   84
116 The top end of South Street   84
117 A 1930s photograph of South Street   85
118 The Lord Mayor of London's procession   85
119 Romford Town Hall, 1960s   86
120 A Class C dwelling in the Modern Homes
     Exhibition   87
121 New houses in Clockhouse Lane   87
122 Romford Carnival procession float, 1930s   88
123 Training of personnel   89
124 Advertisement for an indoor shelter   90
125 The Fire Station   90
126 Rescue workers   91
127 Wartime adverts   92
128 Romford's War Weapons Week   93
129 Parachute mine damage   94
130 Borough Engineer F.V. Appleby   95
131 Garden shelter   96
132 Romford Market, 1950s   96
133 Killwick's of Station Parade   97
134 Collyer's furniture business   98
135 Silcock's Radio advert   99
136 New estate plan   101
137 Children in the library   102
138 Romford Market in the 1950s   103
139 Coronation Summer Fete, 11 July 1953   104
140 South Street in the late '50s   105
141 A view along the River Rom   106
142 House in Como Street   107
143 The former *Woolpack* pub   108
144 The Wedding Gallery building   108
145 Bridge over the Rom   109
146 Inside the former Liberty Two   110
147 Relic of Ind Coope's former brewery   110

ACKNOWLEDGEMENTS

Thanks are due to A.E. Jopson for illustration 35, Mrs B. Nelson for illustration 95 and to Mr B. Smith for illustration 91.

Also to K. Longridge, B. Rider and all those who have taken a photographic interest in Romford and its history.

INTRODUCTION

Because so much of its built heritage has been swept away in recent times, the rich past history of Romford is not very evident today. But a surprising legacy is the persistence of place-names first applied many centuries ago. In the town, the area known as Marshalls, to the north-east of the Market Place, including Marshalls Park School, has descended from an old family name Marescall. William Marescall is mentioned in the Hornchurch Priory documents in A.D. 1189. In fact, a large number of personal names given long ago to the house and land where a family lived recur down to the present. They are so old that in this part of former Essex the apostrophe denoting possession has disappeared from the name. The Mawneys area of Romford was once a manor, and derives from the family of Sir Walter de Manny, the chivalrous knight of Edward III's time, who pleaded for the lives of the burghers of Calais. Pettits Lane, once the site of a house called Great Pettits, formed the family estate of Thomas Petit in 1233-7. Crowlands, on London Road, still applied to a primary school and a playing field, was associated with the family of John Crawland (1480) living near what is still called Crow Lane.

There are other ancient names. The Oldchurch area is so called because the early medieval settlement of Romford with the chapel of St Andrew was located here, some way south of the present town. On the 1696 Stewards Map, the former fields here are called Ruin Meadow and Further and Middle Ruins, indicating that traces of the old town had been evident. Similarly, Risebridge in north Romford once denoted a brushwood bridge or causeway over boggy ground. It appears as Ris(e)brugg(e) in documents of 1230 to 1321.

The Manor of Marks to the west of Romford town became part of the Liberty of Havering, when in 1465 its owner, Urswick, obtained special rights entailed in this honour from the king. Its name is recorded in 1368 as Merkes, from the family of Simon de Merk. This family got its name, according to Reaney, from living on the borders of the forest. Cottons Park in London Road commemorates the family of Nicholas Cotton who died in 1570. The family were of high status in 16th-century Romford affairs. Later members of the family (about eleven are listed) have gravestones in St Edward's churchyard. The site of the house is described by Cornell and Terry as standing near to Mawneys Lane, seen on old maps. Cornell says the earlier house stood nearer London Road, opposite Dog Lane (now Waterloo Road). In the 18th century the house was further west, nearly opposite the old *Sun* public house.

The story of these links with past centuries is revealed in the following pages.

ORIGINS

It is believed that the higher ground to the east, in the Marshalls area, would have afforded a safer habitat to the earliest inhabitants of Romford. The present centre and Market area were under water for considerable periods of time. The River Rom had a history of flooding up to the 20th century. A lagoon here possibly provided fish, and a means of getting about by primitive types of boat. The wildwood all round, typical of Britain and Essex at the time, would have provided its own harvest of animals and edible plants, and even herbs and medicinal plants for curing and healing. It has been suggested by archaeologists that the low hill top of Marshalls was occupied by a British hill camp for defence.

The earliest men in the area would have travelled up the River Rom in dugout canoes. Later, coracles may have been used locally. Nearby Walthamstow has produced evidence of pile dwellings on top of platforms above an early lake. No doubt similar arrangements could have existed at Romford.

Archaeological finds in Romford have surfaced occasionally but have not always been consistently investigated until recent times. A writer in the 1930s commented,

> We shall not be far wrong if we say that a settlement of some sort was in existence at Romford in the Bronze Age, for a few years ago a socketed chisel, a broken sword, and other implements were dug up together with some lumps of the metal, on the site where the town stands today. If so, it is probable that the settlement was reached from London by a very ancient trackway which doubtless led to Colchester, or Lexden, the capital of the British tribe, the Trinobantes.

James Kemble's book *Prehistoric and Roman Essex* lists two sites of interest in Romford: at TQ5185, where palaeolithic handaxes and flint flakes were found on a gravel extraction site; and at TQ493892 (Marlborough Road), an early mesolithic, 6th-century B.C. fortified settlement, and a probable late Iron-Age four-sided enclosure surrounded by ditches.

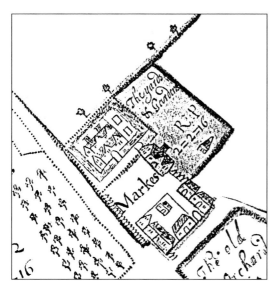

1 *Plan of Marks Manor at the edge of the forest, 1662.*

An especially interesting location is on the upper slopes of Havering Park, north of Romford, where an experienced antiquarian, Bert Hammond, in the 1970s and 1980s, mapped out a huge area of post holes and calculated that the angles of this 'Havering Henge' indicated a direct connection to other significant megalithic sites across England and Europe. These ranged from Callanish in the north to Wandlebury, Avebury, Maiden Castle and Stonehenge, and down to La Gorgue and Carnac in the south and east. Distances between points tied in with the Megalithic Mile proposed by Scottish Professor Thom, who has written about his megalithic theories. Bert Hammond came to the conclusion that Havering might even have been a training ground for the early surveyors and builders of these important sites.

The main road through Romford to East Anglia is a very old road. It is believed that when the Romans came and built what was then a major highway across the Essex wastes it partly followed an even more ancient route. Cutting back the forest to a considerable distance on either side to prevent ambush required a sizeable army of roadbuilders. Many of these were slave labourers driven on by soldiers, both workers and soldiers coming from all parts of the Roman Empire. At opportune moments a worker unable to bear any more would make a break for it, heading into the dense woodland. An efficient search would follow, using trackers with local knowledge, which would usually drag the absconder back to work, for it was not easy to recruit new workers. Undoubtedly some escapees formed small bands of outlaws, living just beyond the reach of Roman rule. There were also communities of native Britons scattered across the thinly populated landscape. Key personnel in these groups were the priesthood of druids. They were not only religious leaders but guardians of culture and traditions. Strange survivals of their customs are still found buried in today's society in superstitions, place-names and words and phrases.

When writers locate Roman 'Durolitum' in the Romford area they are relying on a certain amount of evidence available to us, beginning with the famous Antonine Itinerary, or road book recording the route from London to Colchester and listing the following staging posts:

2 *Lowlands in London Road, as seen by A.B. Bamford, September 1900.*

3 *Ancient dugout canoe recovered from the Thames. Hewn from a solid tree trunk, it is about 18 feet 6 inches long.*

Londinium – Durolitum xv miles
Durolitum – Caesaromagnus
   (Chelmsford)   xvi miles
Caesaromagnus – Canonium
   (Kelvedon)   xv or xii miles
Canonium – Camulodunum
   (Colchester)   viii miles.

Although there exist slightly differing versions of the above, it can be seen that the distance between the stations on the 'Great Road' was generally fifteen miles, a sensible marching distance. Because of the importance of Colchester as the provincial capital of Britain, the first station out from there is approximately half the distance. The Romans tried where possible to take a completely straight course between any two points, so that where the line of the road is lost one can attempt to retrace it, using a ruled line between two known points at either end. The line of the road from London can be traced along a reasonably direct course through Old Ford, Stratford, Forest Gate and Manor Park, with only minor diversions. It continues through Ilford, Seven Kings (where there is a minor diversion today to cross the railway) and Chadwell Heath. From Chadwell Heath, after a slight realignment to the east, it gets to the outskirts of Romford, where London Road now takes a southern course away from what was probably the original path. The line of the road between the western side of Romford and Gallows Corner is off line. From Gallows Corner it sets off straight as an arrow again towards Brentwood. The reason for the diversion may have been problems with flooding at

4 *An early Briton using a coracle.*

5   *An early drawing of the stones of Callanish.*

6   *Coins of the powerful Cunobelin who controlled Essex for 30 years between the two Roman invasions. Coins from continental and eastern civilisations of this era have been discovered in the area, on Gidea Park sports ground for example. It has been suggested that the line of an ancient trading route lay through Romford and early tin traders brought their wares through Essex from Cornwall before shipping them abroad from an Essex port.*

the old ford, and it appears that the new route was constructed across embankments built up on either side of the River Rom to enable a bridge to be built.

The Roman mile was slightly shorter (by about 142 yards) than the English mile, and this seems to place Durolitum in the Gidea Park area. Here, significantly, on the line of the present Main Road to Gallows Corner, is the district known as Hare Street. This gets its name from the Old English word meaning army, and was probably christened by the later Saxons being aware of the remains of Roman occupation of the site. Indeed, this would have been the main street running through the middle of a camp.

Placed at one side of the Roman road, Durolitum was a strategic barracks and posting station placed on the high ground overlooking the ford in the valley of the Rom. It would have stretched northwards towards the line of the original Roman road. An apparent route, of made-up ground across the present golf course, was listed at one time as an Ancient Monument. A similar track appeared in a hot summer across Gallows Corner sports ground. As well as the main camp on the high ground, there would have been settlements and guard posts in the area. Burials, as was customary, have been found away from the site at Hare Street. Finds from the Roman period have cropped up north of the Market Place, on the site of the Dolphin Centre, and in the Cottons Park area, London Road. These were from cremation burials. Associated finds included fragments of lamps, amphorae, cooking pots, tiles, coins and brooches.

Although Durolitum has not been found, stray finds from Roman times have occurred near the centre of the town and in locations within the district that was part of the former Romford borough. At the end of the 19th century, in South Street, a new water main trench cut into decayed woodwork five feet down. This find was only 20 yards away from the High Street and the wood contained seven or eight bronze nails, one of which was described as four inches long and having a head nearly two inches square. Could this structure have been on the approach to Roman works building embankments to bridge the Rom? A section of a large key was also found. The woodwork could, alternatively, have been part of a Roman landing place next to the Rom, the river being wider in those days. Round the corner in the High Street, at a similar time, two brass coins of the Roman period, but worn so as to be illegible, were found at a depth of five feet when workmen were digging a cellar for the rebuilt *Woolpack Inn*. In 1906, when the old bridge over the

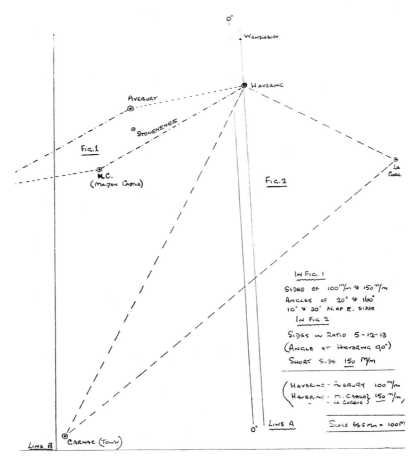

7 *The geometry of Havering's connection to other large-scale megaliths.*

Rom was demolished, a bronze coin of Vespasian emerged from the earth. The Ashmolean Museum in Oxford contains a 'replica' of an as of Caligula found at Romford, location unknown.

Several finds from the countryside around include the base of a Samian ware vessel from Collier Row, bearing the stamp BELSVS FEC, and items from what was apparently a Roman Villa excavated by Harry De Caux. During the enclosures of Romford Common in 1814, in the Noak Hill area, fragments of roof tile, 'over a stretch 300 paces long', were found while laying out a new road one mile north-west of the main London Road. Along the London Road, in the Harold Wood/Harold Hill area, urns, patera and a bottle were discovered 'behind a farm house near the 14th milestone'. The 14th milestone from London is clearly marked on Chapman and André's Map of Essex of 1777.

In about A.D. 410 the last of the Roman soldiers departed across the Channel to try to bolster the Empire against attacks from raiders beyond the borders. The Britons and Romano-Britons who stayed behind did their best to hold onto a culture which they took with them as they retreated towards the West Country and Wales, where they were ruled by a succession of kings. In Essex, Saxon raiders began to establish their own dynasties. Some remnants of the Romano-British population, perhaps those at the Collier Row Villa, may have merged with Anglo-Saxons coming in along the Thames. Saxon settlements were mainly along the Thames

8   *Roman milestones were placed along all main roads.*

9   *Roman pavements like this lay under the ground somewhere in the Romford area. Remains of villas in Collier Row and Rainham have already been found.*

shore, at Rainham, Dagenham, Barking and nearby Mucking, but their success in colonising Essex is evident in the recent discovery of a royal tomb with extremely rich furnishings in the Southend area. The name of nearby Rainham is also believed to have derived from the Anglo-Saxon – place of the ruling people. In 1937 a tremendous hoard of high quality grave goods – shield bosses, spear heads, jewellery, pottery and two glass drinking horns – turned up.

A mystery attaches to the foundation of a royal house or palace on the hill at Havering-atte-Bower, just north of Romford. Like so many others in Essex, the place-name is undoubtedly Anglo-Saxon, but it might have developed from a settlement of the Haeferingas (the people of Haefer, a local leader) to become the retiring place of a king.

10 *Hare Street, seen here in 1880, continued as a place of refreshment on the site of former Durolitum.*

The late George Caunt wrote about the background to the mystery concerning the establishment of Havering Palace: 'So, apart from Edward the Confessor and Harold II, we must look before Alfred for possible royal connections with Havering. The old royal family of Essex reigned from 600-830 with London as the nominal capital. The names of fourteen kings of Essex are known, but it was never an important dynasty, nor was Essex an important kingdom. The last king, Sigered, began as Rex, then sub-regulus, and finally Ealdorman under the King of Mercia. After this there were no more kings of Essex and the dynasty disappeared.' Caunt points out that these shadowy kings would have had wooden halls and palaces in their own territory and, traditionally, one of these might well have been at Havering. Morant, the historian of Essex, says, 'In the Saxon times, it was ancient demesne, of the Crown Imperial of this realm. Havering Bower was an ancient retiring place of some of our Saxon kings: particularly of the simple saint, Edward the Confessor.' Edward had his 'spin doctors', who created the legend of the famous ring given away to a beggar and returned by travellers who said it had been given to them by St John the Evangelist with the news that within six months Edward

11 *Stickleback Bridge, seen here in the early 1900s in a sketch by Leonard Davey, was where the Roman road originally crossed the River Rom.*

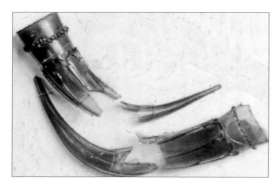

12 *Saxon drinking horns from Rainham, made of green glass, unique in Britain at the time of their discovery in 1937.*

would know the joy of heaven with St John. The sapphire in the top of the Imperial State Crown is said to have come from this ring. Edward was also said to have liked the seclusion of Havering so much that to assist his meditation and prayer he commanded the warbling nightingales among the trees to fly away – after which their song was not heard again in the precincts of the palace. But the birds have returned in heraldic form as the badge of the pupils of St Edward's School, Romford.

The Saxon Kings of Essex

Erkenwin (Erchwine)	c.527
Sledda	587
Sebert (becoming St Sebert)	597
Saxred	614
Sigebert I (Parvus, 'The Little')	617
Sigebert II (Sanctus, 'The Good')	623
Sigebert III	655
Sigeric and Sebba	663
Sigenard	693
Offa	700
Selred	709
Swithred	738
Sigeric	792
Sigered	799-825

13 *Edward the Confessor, Romford and Havering's patron saint, is the man who created lordships of the manor.*

PUTTING ROMFORD
ON THE MAP

When the travellers reported to Edward the Confessor that St John the Evangelist had said he would be in heaven within six months, he gave up his throne to his brother-in-law Harold. The problem was that Edward, who had lived in Normandy with his Norman mother Emma from the age of 10 until he was 35, had promised the throne to William of Normandy in 1051. Harold succeeded to the royal manor of Havering and, in spite of the fact that he could have spent little time in the district, gave his name to Harold Wood. As we know, he was killed by the Normans at the Battle of Hastings in 1066, whereupon William the Conqueror became king. In apportioning out his kingdom to his knights and others, he was aware of the royal status of the manor of Havering and kept it for himself. Twenty years later it was recorded in Domesday Book as 'Haveringae' a place with a population of some 400 persons living in the manor, consisting of the families of 40 villeins, or farmers, 41 bordars, or smallholders and six serfs. It seems that some kind of King's House existed at Havering, for only 47 years after the Conquest Henry I was instructing his scribe to confirm in a document from this location certain liberties in Feering, Essex that were to be granted to Westminster Abbey.

Domesday Book records:

Hundred of BECONTREE
  Harold held HAVERING (atte-Bower) before 1066 as 1 manor, for 10 hides.

Then 41 villagers, now 40. Always 41 smallholders; 6 slaves; 2 ploughs in Lordship. Then 41 men's ploughs, now 40. Woodland, 500 pigs; meadow, 100 acres; now 1 mill.

2 cobs, 10 cattle, 160 pigs and 269 sheep.

Attached to this manor before 1066 were four free men with four hides who paid the customary due. Now Robert son of Corbucion holds three hides and Hugh de Montfort the fourth hide, and they have not paid the customary due since they have had them.

And, besides, Robert also holds four and one half hides which one free man held in this manor before 1066.

Also associated was one free man with 30 acres who paid the customary due; John son of Waleran now holds him. Value of this manor before 1066 £36; now £40; Peter the Sheriff receives from it £80 in dues and £10 in gifts.

To this manor belong 20 acres which lie in Loughton (and) which Harold's reeve held before 1066; now the King's reeve holds them. Value 40d.

Henry I seized the crown while his elder brother Robert was on his way home from the Crusades following the death of William Rufus. Because many of the Norman barons were for Robert rather than Henry, the latter had to rely on the support of the English people, and this resulted in his giving them a charter of liberties. In addition, his wife was a princess descended from the old line of English kings, which meant that royal

14 *Bow Bridge, Queen Matilda's great idea that may have helped to put Romford Market on the map.*

descendants from now on traced their ancestry not only from William I's line, but also from Alfred and the old English kings.

Henry's wife, known both as Matilda and Maud, was the second of three queens proud to number among their achievements their being Abbess of Barking. She also made an impact on travel on the Great Road into Essex through Romford. Because she had, from time to time, to pay visits to her abbey, she made her way out of London through the City wall and gate and followed the route of the old Roman road through 'Old Ford'. There were few bridges at the time, and all travellers had to plunge through the various rivers on horseback, or on foot at a shallower point. Sometimes even a ferry would be needed. When the River Lea was in spate, the Queen was, in the words of an old chronicler, 'well washed' as she attempted the crossing. John Stow recorded in his later history that the Queen 'caused two stone

bridges to be builded in a place one mile distant from the old foord, of which one was situated over Lue [i.e. the Lea] at the head of the town of Stratford, now called Bow, a rare piece of worke, for before that time the like had never been seen in England; the other over the little brooke commonly called Chanelse Bridge [the Channelsea]'. These bridges improved traffic along the Great Essex Road to such an extent that trade and commerce were improved, and eventually it became imperative that a market be established along the line of the road, north of the medieval town of Romford at Oldchurch.

This would have been a significant turning point in the history of Romford. Hornchurch village had previously dominated the local Havering area economy, with its busy trade in hides and skins, because it was the location of the Priory of St Nicholas and St Bernard. Hornchurch had its own through route known as the Royal Road in the early Middle Ages, as it was the chief place of worship in the King's Manor of Havering.

On the banks of the Rom at Oldchurch, near the edge of the huge forest which stretched away northwards mile after mile, and was a jealously guarded hunting preserve, the villagers rediscovered the value of a good natural site. The first appearance of the name Romford is recorded in a document of 1166, which states that Roger Bigod, Earl of Norfolk holds the woodlands of Romford. The villagers were probably employed in several forest trades. One such craft was that of charcoal burning, and the colliers as they were called gave their name to the place Collier Row, further north in the great wood. Many times during the hot summers of the 12th century did the wood catch fire, and it is suggested that this is the origin of the name of Brentwood to the east.

King John, who reigned from 1199 until 1216, was extremely fond of visiting the royal palace of Havering. An interesting record has come down to us of the exact dates on which he visited it in the years between 1203 and 1214. He went hunting on many of these occasions and a letter written by the King to the Earl of Alnwick put in his hands the responsibility for the construction of kennels at Romford in which to house the royal hunting dogs. The factor which really seems to have encouraged the growth of Romford at this time was the renewed interest being shown in the old Roman route to Chelmsford. The road had obviously been given some attention in the way of clearance and repair, fords being improved and even some bridges built. Romford became an outlet for the leather items produced by Hornchurch traders. This had probably started spontaneously, but by 1247 the King had become aware of the

development on his royal manor and ordered the Sheriff of Essex to proclaim its official status in the Close Rolls, the record of royal decisions. This set the seal on Romford's progress and probably led to the founding of extra settlements around the little town. These, together with Romford, Hornchurch and Havering-atte-Bower, were to become, just over two centuries later, the nucleus of the Liberty of Havering. The road through Romford and the new trading encouraged the town to develop northwards from the original Oldchurch site, but this happened gradually. First of all, in 1323, the monks of St Bernard's Priory, Hornchurch obtained permission for a chapel of St Andrew's to be built at Oldchurch. Romford's growing population no longer needed to travel to Hornchurch for their spiritual necessities. They could now bury their dead in Romford rather than carry them to the former place. The church of St Andrew was flooded so often that it followed the trend and moved northwards to a new site beside the Market Place, where a wood was chopped down to be used in the structure. The new church now looked out on the great highway along which everything moved. From time to time, travellers on the road died and were buried within its confines.

A treasure trove of information about Romford's past is stored at New College, Oxford, where hundreds of early documents relate to land deals made when the Priory of St Nicholas and St Bernard was in existence on the hilltop at Hornchurch in the 13th and 14th centuries. At its dissolution, William of Wykeham was able to acquire the lands and documents belonging to the Priory, founding Winchester College and New College, Oxford at this time. An early example of a legal transaction affecting Romford in this collection is the following:

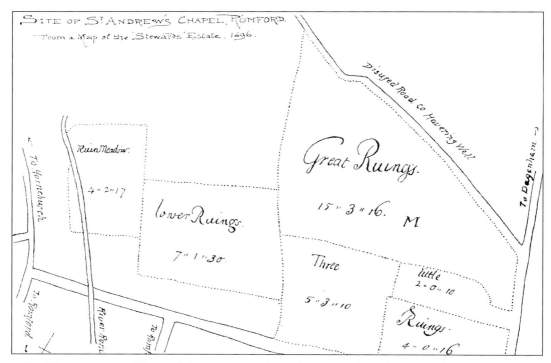

Site of St Andrew's Chapel, Romford.
From a Map of the Stewards Estate. 1696.

15   *The estate map of Stewards Manor (1696) shows the Ruin Fields, where the old town and church of Romford were situated in early medieval times. Oldchurch Road runs along the bottom. In land deeds of 1451 this was Oldechurche Lane. South is at the top.*

Grant from Geoffrey son of William de Solio to Richard de Ulmis of Havering of ground and messuage (dwelling-place) with garden in Havering at Romford, which his father William had, which tenement belongs to the tenement which Richard de Ulmis holds of William Dun. And his father William sold it to Adam Lincolnia who in turn sold it to William Dun. And the said Richard has paid two marks of silver for this grant. Witnesses William Dun, William, son of John de Uphavering, Walter de Wybregge, Elias de Bruera, William Annore, Robert Annore, Geoffrey fitz Peter, Simon de Strata, Adam Goding, Martin Clerk and others. [Document undated but probably from about 1233]

The name de Ulmis is that of the family who later gave their name to a landholding between Romford and Hornchurch which,

combined with another, became the district of Bush Elms. Adam Lincolnia may have been a prosperous merchant of the city of Lincoln. A famous rout occurred there in 1217, when 406 knights, 317 crossbowmen and some attendant men at arms supporting the cause of King John defeated Louis, who later became King of France, and his forces. Although Louis held London and many strong points in Surrey, Sussex and Hampshire, including Winchester, the Romford region was probably untouched. There were few strong points of sufficient strength to be important to invaders in the area. The battle at Lincoln brought civil warfare to a halt and a peace treaty was signed at Kingston.

Other documents in the Hornchurch Priory collection show a really thriving little town, where merchants and others

16 *Shields in Westminster Abbey choir aisles. Being the Arms of the family of Henry III, as mentioned in the Royal Accounts, these designs were mainly duplicated at Havering Palace. The Plantagenet kings spent much time at the Palace. Henry III, particularly, with his excessive devotion to St Edward the Confessor, made Havering one of the principal residences of the kings and queens of England until the close of the 14th century.*

made quick fortunes buying and selling goods. Although housing was growing, one document shows how the town was still surrounded by fields and largely agricultural.

> Acknowledgment Geoffrey fitz Peter of Romford that he is bound to Richard de Havering in a rent of thirty four shillings a year for lands and tenements, to specify – the field called Brodefeld once held by Adam Kori, and the field called Westmad once held by William de Solar, and four acres of land which Roger Pistor once held in the parish of Romford, and the field which is called Melnfeld except the windmill on it ... Item for the whole field Sweynesfield in Havering and the field called Meguage which Simon Thorn once held of the said Richard ... Item for twenty three acres of land in two fields

called Wonfeld and Longfeld ... Item for one messuage in Rumford once held by Simon Thorn.

The reference to Melnfeld and its mill is interesting. Meln is a corruption of the Norman French predecessor of 'moulin', which shows there had been a windmill on the site for quite a number of years.

There were also several watermills on the river through the town and adjacent meadows. In the reign of Henry III, about 1230, one Richard de Dover (after whom Dovers Corner in South Hornchurch is named) held two streams or tributaries of the local river and used them to turn watermills: the 'Mercke-dych', the medieval name of the Rom specified in the original documents, to the bridge at Romford, and another stream to the Abbot of Waltham's

17 *Seal of Simon de Montfort. A 14th-century romance claims that Simon's son, Henry, survived the Battle of Evesham and was nursed by a baron's noble daughter. In fear for his life, he adopted the disguise of 'the silly blind beggar of Bethnal Green'. Bessie, his fair and beautiful daughter, despised for her apparent lowly status, set out along the Essex road to seek her fortune. In the ballad her shabby costume deterred suitors, but at Romford she was treated well, and when she visited an early public house, the* Queen's Arms, *one man took her for his own and her noble origins were revealed. Popular in the Elizabethan age, the ballad seems to show Romford as a place where all classes mixed and anything could happen.*

mill. Richard de Dover paid twelve pence per annum for these streams.

Romford at this time must have had a busy but rural atmosphere, similar to the monk Fitzstephen's account of the northern suburbs of London about the same period. The fact that many properties and pieces of land are recorded as having changed hands in the town during the 13th and 14th centuries indicates that not only was the nucleus of the town growing, but the fields and farms beyond were also hives of activity.

One of the legal records is a bond of Peter de Brenho, master of Hornchurch (Priory) to Thomas Brookman of Rumford in the sum of ten pounds to pay him certain quantities of wheat and oats (dated at Rumford, July 22nd, eighth year of Richard II, i.e. 1384) Peter de Brenor, as he is called elsewhere, was the last but one prior of the religious house of Hornchurch.

A study of the documents concerning the sale and exchange of property, land and varying kinds of 'service' brings us up against the feudal laws of the time. The king, by right of conquest, possessed all the lands in England. He then distributed them to his leading subjects in return for military and other types of service; these favoured chief tenants sub-let their holdings among lesser tenants, usually for further services of various kinds. This could go on even further down the scale so that the structure of land tenure was highly complex. In the upper levels the 'military' service due for a block of land would be the equipping of a knight on horseback for the king's wars and warlike expeditions. An example of payment in money is the following:

> Grant from Richard de Havering to Ralph [?, damaged document – therefore surname or other words are missing] for ten marks of silver of a messuage with curtilage and four acres of land ... Romford in the vill of Havering ... which is between the land of Robert Longwebbe towards ... once of Hugh le Mareschal. Witness – Robert de Chygewell, Bailiff of Havering, Roger Elys, John le Cu, William de Uphavering, Robert, Clerk of Rumford, John de Ulmis and others [undated, but probably about 1269-72].

The reference to Rumford as the vill (or town) of Havering shows its growing importance.

KINGS, QUEENS AND CITIZENS OF THE LIBERTY

The manor of Hornchurch, later Havering, was by the middle of the 15th century a place of some importance. Seizing the opportunity, Thomas Urswick, a courtier, used his influence with King Edward IV to obtain extra powers and rights for what was to be called the Liberty of Havering, including Romford, Hornchurch and Havering-atte-Bower. Urswick even managed to stretch the boundary of the old manor to get his estate of Marks (formerly part of Dagenham) included in the Liberty. This boundary, once

18 *The Havering halfpenny is often described as a token coin redeemable at local businesses. In fact, it is more of a souvenir medalet commemorating the establishment of the Liberty in 1465, which date it bears, although it was apparently issued in the 1790s.*

established, survived for over 500 years until a recent parliamentary boundary change returned the area once known as Marks to Dagenham. The Liberty, Manor or Lordship of Havering-atte-Bower, which divided into Romford side and Hornchurch side, ran down to the Thames between Dagenham and Rainham. Over the centuries, this greater Havering gave its name to Havering Plain, north of Noak Hill, and Havering Well, a district more recently known as Roneo Corner. The Liberty continued until 1892, when it was finally dissolved, although it had lost most of its powers in the 19th century as the town of Romford became more urban.

Harold Smith, historian of Havering and expert on the Liberty, explained the complicated nature of the Liberty and its predecessor, the royal manor:

Havering, in the full sense, was ancient demesne of the kings of England, having come down to them from Edward the Confessor. Inhabitants of ancient demesne enjoyed special privileges; villeins possessed much more freedom than elsewhere, being almost freeholders [protected by the 'little writ of right']. Tenants or inhabitants enjoyed exemption from tolls throughout the land; this was specially recognized in the case of Havering by Edward III, 1368 and Henry VII, 1505 [Patent Rolls]; in the latter case there is also exemption from 'contributing towards the knights coming to Parliament' – exemption from

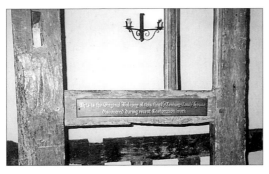

19 *This old framework within the* Golden Lion
*pub survives from a 'fine 15th-century coach
house, discovered during recent restoration
work'. The Charter stimulated the growth of
Romford and this inn, which may have started as
a pilgrim and traveller's hostel sponsored by the
church, was at the centre of much activity.*

payment to MPs ... The Liberty was
not a corporation of the usual type, but
simply a magnified manor. Its history
shows manorial courts at work until quite
recent times. When Elizabeth renewed
the Charter in 1588 she constituted the
tenants and inhabitants a body corporate,
with a common seal. At the time of the
last renewal by Charles II, there was
some talk of assimilation to an ordinary
corporation, with a recorder and town
clerk appointed by the king.

This, of course, never happened, but
Romford finally became a borough with a
mayor in 1937, 45 years after the Liberty
ceased. The freedoms and rights enjoyed
meant that Havering and Romford were
a hundred years ahead of the rest of the
country. It has to be said that some of the
inhabitants took it into their own hands
to extend their privileges and some of the
Royal Forest that existed at the beginning
of the medieval period became private
landholdings – James I discovering that
forest areas had been cut down when he
came to the throne.

The king's palace at Havering was a
retreat for royalty for more than 600 years.

The eminence of Havering Hill, 300 feet
above sea level, provided a panorama over
the Royal Manor and Liberty down to the
Thames and over to Kent. This hill top was
once crowned by substantial buildings which
often housed the consorts and families,
while the king came and went. The last
royal visitor, Charles I, came to the palace
in 1638.

Many changes took place over the
centuries and the record of various building
works survive in State Papers. At various
times great effort and skill was put into
renewing and decorating the buildings. In
1578 John Symonds produced the one known
plan of the 'King's House' on the orders of
Lord Burleigh (William Cecil). His interest
in the district was personal – he had married
Mildred, one of the five daughters of Sir
Anthony Cooke of Gidea Hall, Romford, the
splendid architecture of which was probably
visible below the hill. Here Edward III
invested his child successor, Richard II. In
1397 a conspiracy was hatched at Havering
to murder the Duke of Gloucester (the uncle
of Richard II). Havering also became the
official residence of England's queens,
among them Henry VIII's first three wives.
At first the Queen's residence was called
The Bower, but later it was known as Pyrgo,
which is said to derive from the original
Portgore. Pyrgo became a separate residence
a little way north of the palace.

In the 17th century, after royal visits had
ceased, the building started to deteriorate.
Local people were successful when they
petitioned the crown for continued use of the
larger chapel as their parish church, in 1650,
and this church was rebuilt at least twice up
to the end of the 19th century. A print dated
1833 in the vestry shows a boarded belfry at
the west end with the words 'underneath the
belfry is the only remnant of the princely
pile'. In fact, the Bower House down the hill

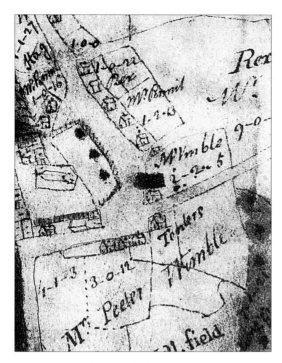

20 *A rare glimpse of the Palace as seen on the Havering Liberty map, c.1618.*

nearer Romford, built in 1729, contains the arms of Edward III sculpted in stone and a remnant of the palace, and many of the houses in the village may rest on foundations of stone removed from the ruins.

With the onset of the Commonwealth period and the palace now in disuse, a survey was made of the possessions of the former royals in 1649-50: 'late parcel of the possessions of Charles Stewart, late king of England; possessed and enjoyed by Henrietta Maria, his queen, in right of her dower … Estimate of rents from tenants and manorial court fees £100.' The tenants of Havering, Romford and Hornchurch claimed their privileges under the Charter, including having a bridge at Romford and the Town Gaol repaired and maintained at the sole cost of the state, and complained that the late king had often disregarded

their privileges. 'All that Manor House of Havering atte Bower with all the outhouses thereunto belonging, set lying and being in the parish of Hornchurch in the county of Essex, being a confused heap of old ruinous and decayed buildings, whose materials of lead, glass, tile, brick, stone and timber, besides the charge of taking of them down and removing them, we value to be worth Four Hundred and Eighty Pounds.' After that the manor gardens and orchard are described and then the parcel of impaled ground commonly called or known by the name of Havering Park. 'All that messuage or dwelling house known as the Great Lodge … the materials of which, the charge of taking them down and removing them being allowed, we value at One Hundred Pounds. All that ruinous tenement called the Little Lodge we value at Forty Pounds.'

The whole manor was divided into four parts and sold. Among the claims on the manor was a very interesting one, in which

The Inhabitants and Parishioners of Havering do clayme the Chapel and Chapel yard lying between the Courtyard on the South Parte and the Gardens of Havering House on the north parte abutting on the Court Yard towards the west and Havering Green towards the east. The inhabitants tender the ensuing reasons for continuance of their enjoyment of the aforesaid chapel and chapel yard.

1 They have quietly enjoyed the Chapel and Chapel Yard for four hundred years last past and have had free access thereunto for divine service without any let or hindrance.

2 Whereas it is alleged that it was the late King's Chapel adjoining and belonging unto his house … This chapel and the ground is separated from the king's house and chapel with a pale, besides the king's chapel has no bells,

21 *Havering Chapel in 1818. The boarded belfry at the west end may have replaced the previous private royal annexe shown on the 1578 plan. The present church is a rebuilt one consecrated in 1878.*

no overseers of the poor, no vicarage house, which this chapel hath and which the inhabitants repaired and re-edified upon their own costs and charges with the assistance of the Vicar of Hornchurch who ought of right to have repaired the same, it being a chapel time out of mind unto Hornchurch … Besides heretofore the Vicar of Hornchurch did every month preach in this Chapel himself and was bound to find a preaching minister and time out of mind the said Vicar did allow and give maintenance towards the minister for the said chapel, and for the further confirmation the inhabitants of Havering and Noke Hill in times past were wont to go their perambulation or procession to continue and distinguish their proper bounds to their wards and this chapel from other wards and chapels.

The decay of the chapel is recorded after this time. With the restoration of Charles II, repairs were perhaps done half-heartedly, but not enough to stop the buildings decaying further. Havering's use as a royal palace was over. Holman's unpublished history of Essex of 1719 records, 'On the top of the hill was the Palace Royal … Tis run to

22 *Old Liberty of Havering symbol. This represents the Palace of Havering but in a portmanteau fashion – a main gate implying there are other buildings behind. Several versions have been used, for the Seal of the Liberty itself, for example, and its predecessors, and by commercial firms in Romford.*

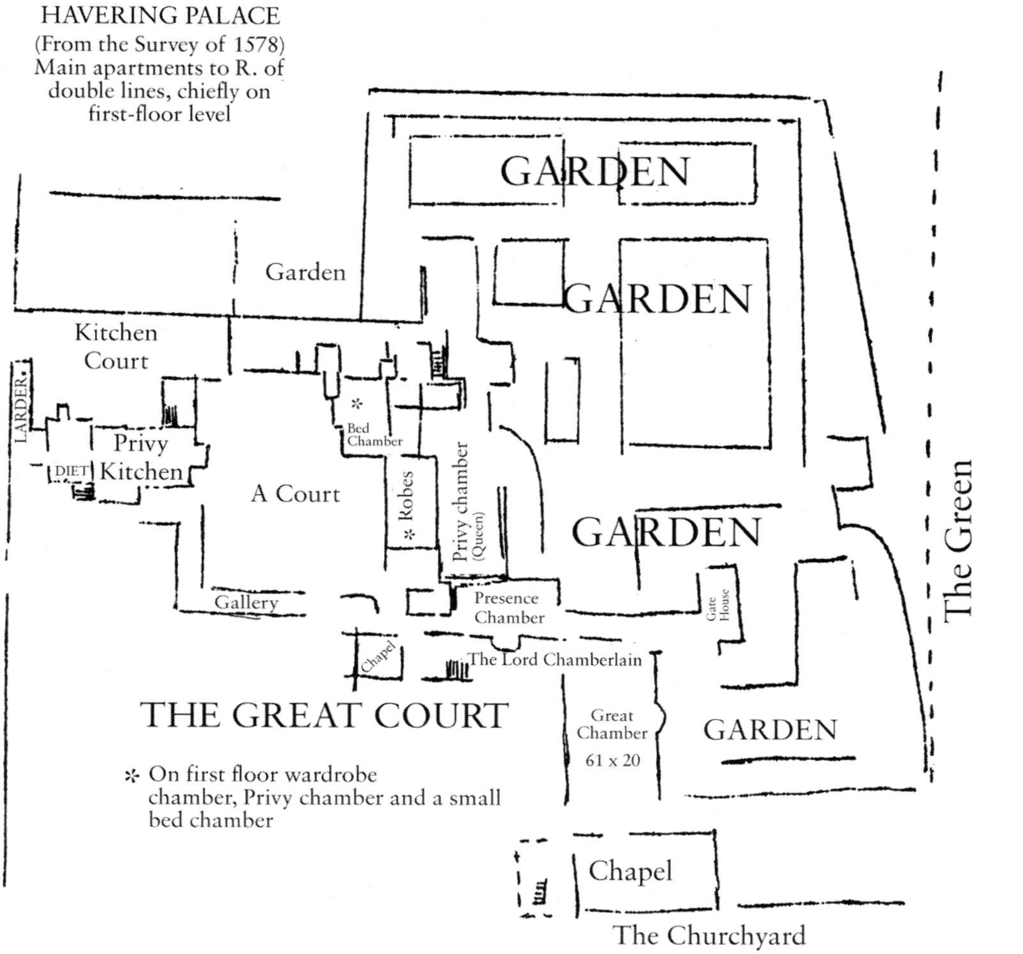
HAVERING PALACE
(From the Survey of 1578)
Main apartments to R. of double lines, chiefly on first-floor level
GARDEN
Garden
GARDEN
Kitchen Court
LARDER
Privy
DIET
Kitchen
Bed Chamber
A Court
Robes
Privy chamber (Queen)
GARDEN
The Green
Gallery
Presence Chamber
Gate House
Chapel
The Lord Chamberlain
THE GREAT COURT
Great Chamber
61 x 20
GARDEN
* On first floor wardrobe chamber, Privy chamber and a small bed chamber
Chapel
The Churchyard

23 *Plan of the former Palace laid over modern features of Havering-atte-Bower village.*

ruin. Twas built of freestone and leaded but now quite uninhabitable.' Salmon wrote in 1740, 'some pieces of the wall of the Royal House are standing but not enough to show the form or extent of it'. Later still, in 1764, Morant's *History of Essex* notes, 'some parts of the wall are still standing but not enough to show its original form or extent it being ruinous and uninhabitable'. Lyson's history of 1796 says, 'that some remains of the palace wall are still to be seen'. Finally, Elizabeth Ogborne in 1816 sounds the death knell, writing, 'part of the wall of the palace continued standing until very lately; but at the present time not a vestige remains'.

When we consider the extent of the palace at its greatest, when it stretched in several directions across the hilltop, with a great chamber between a larger chapel and private apartments containing a smaller chapel, outbuildings from as early as the mid-13th century, and the long two-storeyed building of timber with 26 rooms of 1576, the robbing of the stonework in the latter days must have been continuous and very efficient. Henry VIII had frequently visited the palace at a time when the crown certainly got good value out of the location. Having completed a treaty with France, the King received four French hostages as a guarantee that its conditions would be met. Queen Katherine of Aragon was at Havering, and she asked Henry to bring the hostages when he visited the palace. Katherine hosted a sumptuous feast which was highly praised by the King and the French. In the words of a chronicler, 'The King lying there did shoot, hunt and run with the hostages, to their great joy.' Between 16 and 24 October 1531 Henry touched a poor woman for the King's Evil, carrying on the tradition that English sovereigns had the power to cure this disease.

Henry VIII's two daughters, Mary and Elizabeth, spent some time at Pyrgo. Prince Edward was at Havering, two foreign ambassadors saying that he was 'the prettiest child they ever saw'. Later, some members of the Privy Council visited Edward at Havering when he was ten years old. The King and Prince were both at the palace in September 1542 and were described as 'being merry'. In that year a Privy Council meeting was held at the palace each day between 13 and 21 September. When she became Queen, Elizabeth I was a prolific visitor to Havering. We hear all about this in Nicholl's Progresses, although this is not always a reliable guide. The Queen visited Havering on Tuesday and Wednesday 15 and 16 July 1561, descended on Loughton Hall on 17 July with her retinue, was back at Havering on 18 July, and travelled on to Ingatestone on the 19th.

In Elizabethan times the small town of Romford was ringed by the houses of politically powerful families. Such families could expect the Queen to descend upon them for one or two days' entertainment when she embarked on one of her progresses. Included among these families

24 *Elizabeth I in her glory was seen in Romford on her 'Progresses'.*

were the Cookes of Gidea Hall and so when Elizabeth came to Romford it was not to the palace but to Gidea Hall. Sir Anthony Cooke was a famous scholar and royal tutor. His eldest daughter had married the Lord High Treasurer Burleigh; his second daughter was the wife of Sir Nicolas Bacon, Keeper of the Great Seal, which meant that she was the mother of Sir Francis Bacon, the greatest philosopher of his day; the third daughter married into the influential Russell family, and his fourth was the wife of Sir Henry Killigrew. Elizabeth's visit involved the ordering of large quantities of provisions and other items, enough to bankrupt the less wealthy among the chosen hosts.

Parish registers introduced at this time followed the custom of European countries. In France there were registers as early as 1308, and in Spain Cardinal Zimenes, Archbishop of Toledo, ordered the keeping of registers in every parish in 1497. The earliest parish registers in England were decreed in 1538 during Henry VIII's reign. By the third year of Elizabeth I's reign St Edward's Church in Romford had begun a register. Many of the entries had curious notes attached to names:

Burials

1570 Thomas Browne vocat Quacke Browne [perhaps an unlicensed doctor?]

1574 Robertus Cottonus – goonne powder [result of an explosion?]

1604 A poore woman died in Mawnes Barn [the only shelter she could find?]

1605 Ould Father Giles

1610 Ollyver, a prison'r executed and buryed [on the gallows at Gallows Corner?]

1612 Dumb Joan fm Hare Street

1625 A woman whom they called madd megg.

25 *This once splendid house, the Retreat, lay hidden behind Romford Market frontages. It probably dated from Elizabethan times and remained until the middle of the 20th century, when it was demolished – another victim to the tide of modernisation that suddenly swept through Romford from the late 1960s.*

1626 Toby Asser, killed in a chimney [sent up to sweep it?]

1698 Richard Radley, a stranger, buried naked [no money for the funeral?]

Baptisms

1610 Joshuah Savadge, the son of a condemned woman in prison.

1682 Hagar, a posthumous daughter of Jeffrey Pallmer, late of Romford, who hanged himself.

1768 Edward Shambles, a deserted child, named from the place where he was left [the Shambles were permanent meat storage huts located in front of the church wall for many years].

In 1599 Will Kemp, an actor who belonged to a theatrical company known as The Lord Chamberlain's Servants, made a wager to morris dance from London to Norwich in nine days. He had taken part in performances of plays by Shakespeare and Ben Jonson. Setting off from Whitechapel before 7 a.m. on the first Monday in Lent, accompanied by Thomas Slye on the pipe and tabor and a small group of followers, he describes his approach to Romford at the end of the first day:

From Ilford by moonshine I set forward, dancing within a quarter of a mile of Romford; where in the highway, two strong jades [having belike some great quarrel to me unknown] were beating and biting either of other; and such through God's help was my good hap, that I escaped their hoofs, both being raised with their forefeet over my head, like two smiths over an anvil.

There being the end of my first day's morris, a kind gentleman of London, lighting from his horse would have no nay but I should leap into his saddle. To be plain with ye, I was not proud, but kindly took his kindlier offer, chiefly urged thereto by my weariness; so I rid to my inn in Romford.

26 'In the name of God Amen', the will of John Herde of Collier Row, 1556. On this copy, written into a volume, the scribe has doodled a figure of a man dressed in the high fashion affected by the 'gallants' of the time. He wears doublet, high collar, laced ruff and bombasted hose (stuffed with hair), together with a cap.

27 This old courtyard lying east of the main Gidea Hall appears to be part of an earlier Tudor house on the same site. It was pulled down, with Gidea Hall itself, in 1930.

28 *The rear view of an Elizabethan house still standing in Romford Market Place in the late 19th century under the name 'London House'. Alfred Bennett Bamford was able to record a great variety of ancient structures remaining in Romford at this time. Many of these were inns that for several centuries had catered for travellers on the Great Essex Road.*

29 *Did Will Kemp lodge here? A view from the yard of the* Swan, *an historic inn in Romford's Market Place, drawn by Bamford in 1889. It had changed very little over the centuries.*

Will Kemp rested for two days at Romford, 'being much beholden to the townsmen for their love'. Going back to where he had stopped, he danced through Romford the next morning. Unfortunately he strained his hip at 'Romford town's end', but cured it, although it gave him pain, by continuing to dance on along the road!

Francis Quarles' poetry was a staple volume in many households for two centuries. His family owned the estate of Stewards, which extended from South Street in Romford to Balgores Lane and the Drill Corner in Gidea Park. Much of Romford's shopping centre extends over the site of the original house and nearby grounds. Francis was born at Stewards in

1592 and achieved considerable fame in his day. Although a Royalist, he had a rather Puritan turn of mind, shown clearly in his works which are mostly religious and tend to deal with Hell rather than Heaven. Two of his best known works are 'A Feast of Worms' and, especially, 'Emblems', which went through many editions. Somehow he was always in financial difficulty. His problems were partly caused perhaps by his being a younger son with little inheritance from his father, and partly by the fact that he himself was father to at least 18 children, 13 of whom survived. Quarles died in 1644, leaving mainly a store of witty aphorisms and observations on life, of which the following is an example:

What heere wee see is but a Graven face.
Onely the shaddow of that brittle case
Wherin were treasur'd up those Gemms, which he
    Hath left behind him to Posteritie. *Al: Ross.*
W·M *sculp:*

30 *Portrait of Francis Quarles with poem and symbolic references.*

My Soul, sit thou a patient looker-on;
Judge not the play before the play is done;
Her plot has many changes, every day;
Speaks a new scene; the last act crowns the play.

Sir Anthony Cooke, the royal tutor, lived mainly at Gidea Hall during the middle of the first half of the 16th century, where he brought up his remarkable children, his daughters becoming the most learned women of their time and marrying into important families. Sir William Haddon, in an address to the University of Cambridge, mentioned his visit to the Hall with the comment, 'And what a house did I find there! Yea, rather a small University.' In the next century the house was visited again by royalty in the shape of Queen Marie. By this time, the male line of the Cookes having died out in 1635, the estate and Hall had passed to one of the co-heiresses, Ann Cooke, who had married Sir Edward Sydenham in 1629. Sir Edward was at the court of Charles I, which explains why the house was chosen to break

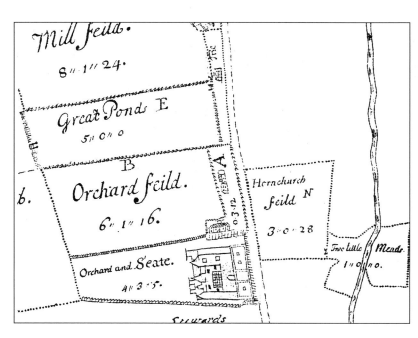

31 *Stewards Manor from the 1696 estate plan.*

32 *Marie de Medici leaves Gidea Hall for London in 1638 as drawn by La Serre, a French courtier who accompanied her.*

Marie's journey from the continent. Charles had met her at Chelmsford and escorted her to Gidea Hall where, in Le Serre's account, she was 'magnificently entertained in that beautiful house'. Le Serre's is the only known illustration of the Tudor Gidea Hall. The building was demolished in 1720 and a more modest mansion erected on the same site by Sir John Eyles, who became Lord Mayor of London.

As the country descended into civil war at the end of the 1640s, Royalists marched along the Romford road, arriving in the town after passing through Ilford and Chadwell Heath on a Wednesday night in June 1648. There is an account of the arrival of General Goring's troops in Terry's *Memories of Old Romford*. The inhabitants of the town were thrown into consternation by the sudden arrival of a body of horse and foot which took possession of the place. They had feathers in their turned up hats or caps, their hair was long and their apparel was loose and not in the best order. They were the remains of the unsuccessful army of the Earl of Norwich which had come from Kent, crossing the Thames the best way they could, often swimming their horses in order to join the Royalists at Chelmsford. They were being chased from Bow by the Parliamentary troopers of the stern Colonel Whalley. Whalley had only given up the pursuit to wait for General Fairfax. The Royalist soldiers spent a sleepless night in Romford. Marks Manor House was attacked by the Royalists and

Carew Hervey Mildmay, a colonel in the Parliamentary army preparing to join his regiment, had to escape from a back window of one of the towers, crossing the moat and plunging into the forest towards Marks Gate. Scarcely had the Royalist troops left Romford the following day than in clattered the pursuing forces of the Parliamentary party under General Fairfax. These troops were distinguished by their high crowned hats, leathern bands armed with pistols, long rapiers under a loose cloak and large leather boots.

In 1643 Oliver Cromwell's rule was enforced through County Committees which were ordered to sub-divide. The division for Southern Essex, usually known as the Romford Committee, included the Hundreds of Chafford and Barstable, the Half-Hundred of Becontree and the Liberty of Havering. The area contained 170,000 acres of forest, marsh and farmland between West Ham and Canvey Island. For a time meetings were held at Brentwood but within months the market town of Romford was chosen as an alternative location. The favourite day for meetings was Thursdays, usually weekly but sometimes at longer intervals, although the original injunction stipulated a twice-weekly meeting. Diane Spivey writes in a study on the work of the Committee,

> the leading County gentry, Sir William Hicks, Sir William Rowe and Sir Henry Holcroft, spent more time away from Romford, especially during the early stages of the war, whilst others, for example Carew Mildmay

33   *A view of Marks Manor, with a tower and a magnificent moat, before it was pulled down in 1808. The book* Secret Hiding Places, *by Allan Fea, states that the demolition, after many years of neglect and decay, revealed a structure complete with hollow walls.*

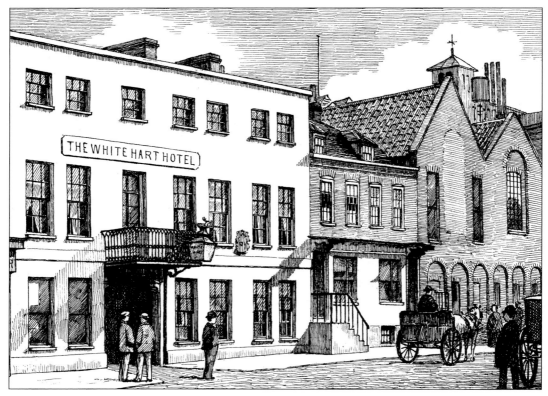

34 *The old* White Hart. *In 1692 an advertisement appeared in the* London Gazette: *'The White Hart to be let; being a very fair, large Inn, with good stables, yard and garden.' During the Commonwealth period, committees were set up throughout Britain, and from November 1643 until 1650 the Romford Southern Divisional Committee met at the* White Hart, *probably because of the good accommodation for man and horse.*

and William Toppesfield, devoted all their attention ... The average size of the committee was ten members ... Procedure followed traditional methods of local administration and resembled the Court of Quarter Sessions. Few of the members were native to the county, and apart from Hicks and Rowe, most were from the middle rank of the gentry ... The committee gradually fell under the domination of two members, John Fenning, a man of inferior social status, and Joachim Mathews, a young newcomer. Much of the work was raising money for Parliament and also fulfilling the need for arms, horses, and men to serve in the military. On August 7th 1643, as an example, Will Peyton wrote to Barrington, 'Having received from the constable a warrant to appear with a lance-horse completely furnished, he desires to be excused, having only £80 per year and having neither horse-furniture nor money to pay for them.'

FASHIONABLE TIMES

The excavation in 1984 of the top end of the market place revealed how the market had grown to twice its original size by the beginning of the 18th century. The eastern end of the market had been open ground until the 15th century. From the middle of the 16th century a large area on the north side and south of the present ring road was used for industrial purposes and especially for the curing of leather hides and skins. A ditch channelled large amounts of water from springs rising behind the present Library and Town Hall into the complex, the waste water being drained into the Loam Pond at the top end of the market. The tannery seems to have continued until about the middle of the 17th century. At this time, its vats, troughs and ditches were dismantled and infilled with rubbish. The site was afterwards levelled with layers of clay and the market extended over it.

The report of the excavation notes, 'In the 18th century, another change appears to have taken place with the erection of a row of timber and brick houses which fronted on to the market. These were to last with some modifications until the 1950s when they were demolished to make way for an open area.' I believe that some demolition took place before this time. In the Second World War bomb shelters occupied part of the site. The report continues, 'The ground plans and the series of brick drains are all that remain of these 18th-century houses, but it is clear that

35 *This token for the* Sun Inn, London Road, *issued in 1657, was the predecessor of those issued by local tradesmen up to the end of the 18th century in order to combat the shortage of official coinage available from the Royal Mint. In the 1790s this situation was finally redressed by Boulton and Watt's issue of the cartwheel pennies and tuppennies.*

36   *Bowling along the road in a stage-coach, a familiar sight in Romford.*

their occupants were at least able to afford certain luxury items since the associated cesspits and rubbish pits contained Venetian glass, Chinese porcelain and Dutch, German and Spanish pottery ... Another interesting find was a chalk mould for making tokens (a type of substitute for coins) ... the bulk of the finds, however consist of fragments of locally made earthenware vessels, building materials and animal bones.'

In 1721 the main road through the town became a turnpike road regulated by Act of Parliament. The great age of stage-coaches began as the improved road surface enabled smoother and faster progress to destinations such as Chelmsford, Colchester and the port of Harwich. The pace of life speeded up. Over the centuries travellers of all kinds had travelled this way out of necessity, as there were few alternatives, so controversy was created when a toll-gate was set up at the eastern end of the market, causing some people to consider that the town was now a prison. The countryside started beyond the toll-gate and the town ended, but new features were beginning to appear along the road. Sir John Eyles pulled down old Gidea Hall and put up a plainer version in 1720. The inns in both Romford and the hamlet of Hare Street to the east grew a little

37   *Carrier's cart.*

with the prosperity brought by better road conditions. Beyond Hare Street, Gallows Corner with its warning gibbet and bridge over a stream gave access to an open area then known as Romford Common. In 1758 Romford races were run on the common north of the present corner. The next year the Western Battalion of the Essex Militia, an early version of the Territorial Army, was reviewed on the common by the Earl of Rochford, Lord Lieutenant of Essex. In addition, the common was known to host the occasional noblemen and others who had decided to fight a duel.

A charity school set up in temporary premises in 1710 had, in 1732, erected a fine premises just inside the toll-gate. The Turnpike Trust produced new strip-maps showing the course of their roads, important features along them, byroads, and details of the owners of land alongside. The improvements to the road helped the traditional carriers whose wagons could be relied on to bring goods to the doors of inns, farmhouses and country cottages. The service was vital to many marooned down difficult byways. The names of carriers appear in the earliest directories towards the end of the 18th century, but they had always been two or three in towns like Romford.

Passenger coaches had also increased in number and details of where they could be boarded were now more publicly advertised. In *New Remarks of London ... collected by the Company of Parish Clerks*, a volume printed by E. Midwinter at the Looking Glass and Three Crowns in St Paul's Churchyard, London, 1732, we learn that the 'Rumford coach leaves the King's Arms, Leadenhall Street on Monday, Tuesday and Thursday each week.'

It is fascinating to think that Romford Common might have developed into another Newmarket. *Patterson's Roads* of 1796 confirms that there was a kind of grandstand and pavilion available: 'Beyond Mr Benyon's Park (Gidea Hall) on left on the Common is a white house, built to see the Races from.'

In spite of its improved road connections Romford was still a parochial enclave in the eyes of some suspicious local inhabitants in 1750. The Romford Bowling Green Club members were jealous of their reputation, and when Dr Johnson's periodical *The Rambler* began to be published in weekly parts and was, presumably, brought to the town aboard a horse-drawn vehicle, there was some kind of sensation. Several of them felt they had been guyed or portrayed in jest.

38   *Old houses on the High Street, Romford. It is 1905 but little has changed for 200 years.*

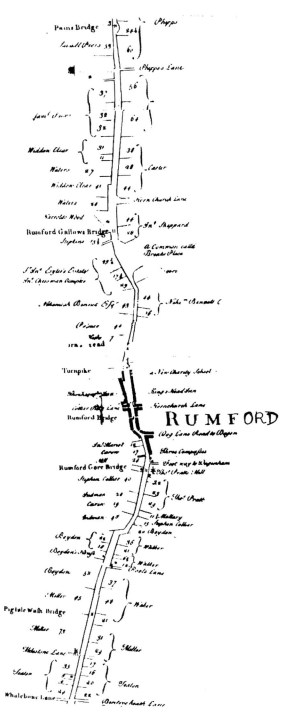

39 *Strip plan of the turnpike road of the 18th century.*

One day it was the character of 'Leviculus', the fortune hunter, then 'Tetrica', the old maid, then an account of a person who spent his life hoping for a legacy, and in another issue someone who is always prying into other folk's affairs. The local gentlemen began to think that one of their number had sat down to divert himself by giving the public a portrait of all the rest. Filled with wrath against the traitor of Romford, they resolved to write to the printer and enquire the author's name. Samuel Johnson was the reply. No more was necessary, for Samuel Johnson was the name of the curate of Romford church. As it was put at the time, 'Soon did each begin to load him with reproaches for turning his friends into ridicule. In vain did the guiltless curate protest his innocence; one was sure that 'Olieger' meant Mr Twigg and that 'Cupidus' was but another name for neighbour Baggs, till the poor parson, unable to contend any longer, rode to London and brought them full satisfaction concerning the writer, who from his own knowledge of general manners, quickened by a vigorous and warm imagination, had happily delineated, though unknown to himself, the members of the Bowling Green Club.'

Present-day Raphael Park with the Gidea Park Garden Suburb still adjoining owes much to alterations made by gentlemen owners in the 18th century. In 1720 a new Gidea Hall building of Georgian design and three storeys high was built by Sir John Eyles, who had demolished the old house two years previously. The old formal gardens were no longer visible from the front side of the building. Eyles had espoused the new parkland panorama so desired by 18th-century landowners. It is not known who the architect was, although there are designs for chimneypieces in the Victoria

40 *Would any of the members of the Bowling Green Club have been sufficiently friendly with the owner of Gidea Hall, Mr Benyon, who had acquired the Hall in 1745, to have visited him there? This view is from a drawing by Humphry Repton of 1794.*

and Albert Museum done by Christopher Cass (1678-1734) which are thought to relate to Gidea Hall. Eyles was also responsible for the lakes in the park. From 1745 the estate was in the hands of the Benyon family. Considerable improvements were made, the house being altered and remodelled by, it is thought, the Adam brothers. The façade was reconstructed with large bow windows, creating oval-shaped rooms behind. In 1797 the Hall was again put up for sale and a summary of the estate follows:

The House, Offices, yards, Bowling Green
and Wilderness (16-3-0)
2 Shrubbery and ponds (5-0-1)
3 Garden (3-2-8)
4 Kitchen Garden field (9-1-16),
5 Vineyard (22-12-6)
6 Canal in Vineyard (2-0-24)
7 Formerly Ozier Ground
   and pond (3-2-6)
8 Oxleys (10-3-30)
9 Shrubbery and Canal
   adjoining (5-0-13)
12 Canal (4-3-13)

41 *Photograph of Gidea Hall in about 1908. Written on the reverse is, 'The Winter Gardens, Chapel, etc. are not shown here but are to the right of the picture – these date back 400 years.'*

(309)

Anno Septimo & Octavo
Gulielmi III. Regis.

An Act for Repairing the Highways between the City of *London* and the Town of *Harwich* in the County of *Essex*.

Whereas the greatest Part of the Highway, between Shenfeild and Ingateftone Town, and between Kelvedon and Stannaway, commonly called Domefey Road., and from Stirwood to Harwich, being Part of the Ancient Highway and Poſt Road, Leading from London to Colcheſter, and ſo to Harwich aforeſaid ; and alſo of the Road between Colcheſter aforeſaid and Langham, called the Severalls ; and alſo the Road called Bulmer Tye and Armſey Road in Bulmer, Leading to Ballingdon in the County of Eſſex, by reaſon of the great and many Loads which are Weekly drawn through the ſame, are become very Ruinous and almoſt Impaſſable, inſomuch that it is become very Dangerous to all perſons that paſs thoſe Ways ; and for that the Ordinary Courſe Appointed by the Laws and Statutes of this Realm is not Sufficient for the Effectual Repairing and Amending the ſame, neither are the Inhabitants of the ſeveral

Iiii   ral

42 *Act of William III for repairing the highways between London and Harwich on the Great Essex Road.*

Several other fields, parklands and lands let out to others are mentioned, as well as four houses in Hare Street Village, with a Wheeler's shop.

An Act of 1555 had tried to ensure that the main roads of Essex were well maintained but it was another 140 years before an attempt was made to deal with problems of maintenance on the road from London to Colchester. An Act of 1695 setting up a turnpike across the road at Mountnessing was the start of a chain of improvements. Before the advent of mail

coaches, post was carried between towns by 'postboys'. These seasoned retainers of the state had to contend not only with bad roads but also with robbers. In September 1693 'the Harwich postboy was set on by five horsemen near Rumford, but there being a gentleman with him, he shot one of them dead, on which the other four fled'. Postboys had also to contend with a plethora of official notices, cautions and warnings from the governors of the mail service, one of whom, the Postmaster General appointed in 1739, was none other than Sir John Eyles of Gidea Hall. William Pitt while Prime Minister realised that the country needed a more efficient mail service and John Palmer of Bath was allowed to try out a new system of mail coaches which cut the time between Bristol and Bath to London in 1784. This led to a new organisation being set up by Pitt, against strong opposition from the Postmaster General and other officials, which was being employed on the Great Essex Road by 1785.

The new mail service was notified to the public in editions of the *Norfolk Chronicle* of 5 March 1785, which stated that the service was by government authority and was guarded and lighted. So it was that, on Friday 25 March, the first service coach set off from the Post Office in Lombard Street in

43 *An old sketch of an early postboy.*

44   An early 19th-century view of the 1410 Church of St Edward's, demolished in 1847 and replaced by the present building. The c.1480 building on the right still remains. but the barns behind are gone.

45   The Cock and Bell Inn, *Romford, built in the 15th century. In 1785 it was described as the principal inn as well as the Post Office run by Isaac Palmer: 'The (post) bag to London goes by the Norwich mail early in the morning.'*

the City at 8 p.m., travelling through the night via Romford, Colchester and Ipswich. The next Monday, 28 March, the mail coach left Norwich at 4 p.m., running via Colchester, Chelmsford and Romford to London and arriving at 8 a.m. the next morning. The cost of travelling by mail coach to Norwich from London was £1 11s. 6d. and the mail carried four passengers compared with the original stage-coach carrying six passengers inside at £1 8s. and anything up to ten outside at 14 shillings. The first lists of coaches going up to London, or down from London, were produced, and woe betide 'any driver of wagons or other person [who] by his Carelessness injure or impede the said carriages by not turning out of the Road on notice being given them'. This official caution must have caused problems for sleepy wagon drivers on Romford roads who were used to letting the horse find its way along the road while they dozed.

POSTMASTERS OF ROMFORD
1674 R. Spicer
1685 A. Wright
1687 Richard Amos
1690 John Chapman
1699 William Jefferson
1709 Mrs A. Winter
1721 John Chapman
1723 William Farre
1742 Katherine Adams

46 *The coach trade had brought many fashionable shops to Romford. A clockmaker by the name of William Smithfield was operating in 'Rumford' in about 1750.*

1760 Thomas Moulton
1766 John Atkinson
1768 Thomas Cook
1781 Isaac Palmer
1790 A. Bramston Snr.
1799 A. Bramston Jnr.

Romford was thriving in the mid-18th century and a few items of local news found their way into what was then the regional newspaper, the *Norwich Post*. In 1764 the *Chelmsford Chronicle* began and it continues as the *Essex Chronicle*. In 1700 the following was reported:

> Stolen the 21st instant out of Mr John Gooch's Ground, of Romford in Essex, a brown Gelding, 7 or 8 years old …

15 Hands high, a Star in his Forehead, all his Paces, he has been anointed with Oyls and Rowell'd for a Stifel on his off Thigh and the Hair not well grown again. Whoever secures him and gives notice to the aforesaid Mr Gooch, shall have a Guinea Reward, and reasonable charges.

In 1761 there was a smallpox scare at Romford. The *Ipswich Journal* of 8 August 1761 contained the following statement, under the names of the Curate, three Churchwardens, three Overseers, two doctors and the Vestry Clerk:

> Whereas it is confidently reported that some evil-minded people have set it forth in this County that the Smallpox still

47   *Queen Charlotte and where she landed at Harwich, 7 September 1761.*

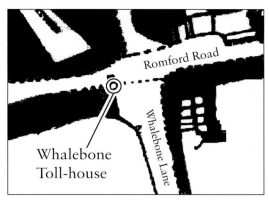

Whalebone Toll-house

48 *The Whalebone toll-gate, a notorious spot for robberies. Even the toll-house was raided on a number of occasions.*

49 *A mid-19th-century view of Romford toll-gate – the only known photo from the north-east. This also shows the top of St Edward's Hall and the posts and rails surrounding the gate.*

rages in the Town of Romford to the great Detriment of the inhabitants there; We whose Names are underwritten, do certify that the Smallpox is entirely ceased in the said Town of Romford.

Presumably the rumour had affected the traders and the market to some extent. Business in local inns probably improved when Princess Charlotte of Mecklenburgh-Strelitz came through Romford at about 12 o'clock on 8 September 1761. She stopped to take coffee at the old 'Queen's House', as it was called from then on. This substantial house stood in the High Street opposite the *Woolpack Inn*. The King's Coach met her here and she proceeded on her journey from Harwich to London to marry George III.

Citizens journeying along the Great Essex Road, especially the wealthier ones, were always liable to be waylaid by persons intent on relieving them of their valuables. The improvements made by the turnpike authorities had not necessarily brought greater security for the individual. Two hot spots in this regard were old Gallows Corner, which was quite an open and lonely spot, and the neighbourhood of the Whalebone Turnpike on the London side of Romford. The gibbet or gallows positioned at Gallows Corner was meant to deter highwaymen, by showing the awful consequences of the deed, but by 1730 executions seem to have gone out of fashion. It is not known when the last took place. The gallows was in a ruinous state until it was repaired in 1785. By 1815 it was called the 'old gallows' and was no longer in use. In 1769 there was a hold-up of the Norwich Post Coach, 'near the Gallows'. A young highwayman robbed one of the passengers of two guineas and another of thirty shillings. In 1752 it was reported that several coaches and carriages were robbed 'near the Whalebone, on the road to Rumford, by a single Highwayman, exceedingly well-mounted'. It was, generally, still safer to travel by coach or in a group.

Kent's Assistant for 1788 gives details of coaches passing through Romford in the course of a day. First of all came the Norwich coach carrying the mails. This left the *White Horse*, Fetter Lane late every evening, calling at Romford, Chelmsford, Colchester and other towns in East Anglia. Another coach, from the *Three Nuns*, Aldgate, started out for Romford every afternoon at three in the summer and two in the winter. From the *Saracen's Head*, Aldgate a coach left daily at four in summer and two in winter. What was called a 'Caravan' left the *Bull*, Aldgate on Wednesday and Friday mornings at six, and a wagon travelled on Tuesday, Wednesday and Saturday mornings at nine.

Cases brought up at the Havering Liberty Quarter Sessions shed light on riotous times in Romford. In 1776 at the Epiphany Session there was a case of assault by an official. It was stated that on Monday night last, being 23 October, John Hulme of Great Warley, yeoman, was assaulted by John Davies, one of the toll collectors at Romford, who struck the examinant near the said turnpike gates with his hand a blow on the face. Thomas Finch, also one of the toll-keepers at Romford Gate, collared the informant and struck him twice with his hand and refused to let the informant

50   *The house in North Street, Romford, which had once been the residence of Marmaduke Grafton's important family, was drawn in 1889 by A.B. Bamford but had not changed significantly over several centuries.*

pass through the said toll-gate though the informant tendered him the toll. Yet another witness, John Bailey of Romford, labourer, 'on oath saith … that on Monday last … he was violently assaulted and beaten by William Perry, servant to (none other than) Isaac Palmer (the Postmaster) of Romford aforesaid, and that the said William Perry then kicked him, the said John Bailey, and seized him by the collar and drag'd him to the cistern in the yard of the said Isaac Palmer and gave him a violent blow on the head'. There were a number of cases of profane swearing. In 1800 an entry in the register runs: 'Be it remembered that on the 24th day of September in the fortieth year of His Majesty's Reign (George III) Richard Lee of Romford, gardener, was convicted before me (Marmaduke Grafton) of swearing one profane oath.' Grafton, acting as the Justice on this day, came from a very old Romford family.

The civil parish of Romford was created in 1786 from one of the ward divisions of the older Hornchurch parish, so as to improve the method of dealing with paupers. From now on the Poor Law was to be administered in Romford by a body of 30 prominent men, to be known as Directors or Guardians, chosen from those rated for this purpose at £10 or over. Committees of three were to carry out the superintending of the Poor

Law at any one time, working in rotation. The Act putting this into effect opened with the words:

> Whereas the present workhouse in the parish of Romford is not sufficiently large and convenient for the Reception and Employment of the Poor of the said Parish. And Whereas it would tend to the better Relief and Employment of the Poor, and be of Benefit to the Inhabitants of the said Parish, if a commodious Workhouse was provided therein and proper powers given for governing, maintaining and regulating the Poor of the said Parish.

The Directors named were as follows: Richard Benyon, George Nicholls, Humphry Repton, John Arnold Wallenger, Richard Neave, William Dearsly, John Tyler, Henry Goody, William Morris, William Gann, Nathaniel Hayward, Isaac Palmer, Job Tipper, Thomas Chubb, John Steary, John Marmaduke Grafton, Thomas Talbot, John Hill, William Gibling, William Barnes, James Trott, Thomas Day, Cuthbert Mashiter, Moses Barham, Abraham Delamare, William Hawes, John Lowry, Edward Thomas Carder, Henry Stace and John Keeves, together with the Churchwardens of the said Parish for the time being.

Some of these men we have already come across, such as Richard Benyon of Gidea Hall, or John Marmaduke Grafton

52   *The Round House, an elegant and ingenious building said to have been built by a tea dealer in 1794, but possibly earlier, still stands in Havering-atte-Bower.*

acting as Justice. The Delamares ran a gentlemen's boarding school in the town and Abraham is an ancestor of Walter de la Mare, the poet. Cuthbert Mashiter is a member of the family after whom Mashiters Walk was named. Isaac Palmer, we have seen, was the Postmaster, and John Arnold Wallenger lived at Hare Hall Mansion, which today forms part of Royal Liberty School. Humphry Repton we will come across shortly.

A foreign tourist who left a diary called *Sophie in London* came through Romford in 1786 and commented, 'how refreshing the country was from Ingatestone here! Everything cultivated: trees and meadows everywhere most gloriously green; and Romford, oh how sweet! Wide streets with a little garden ten paces long in front of each house on the street side; not childishly laid out with cockles and mussels or trimmed box – oh no! – but planned with tasteful

economy, on the fine lawn a large bush of flowers or else shrubbery; in one part stands a basket of flowers with paths running beside it, on another a vase is placed on a hillock covered with flowers, or a group of two boys playing among the wonderful verdure; the path leading to the steps neatly inlaid with marble tiles or Portland stone, the whole surrounded by light well wrought trellis work.'

A Directory of the 1780s says that Romford had three markets weekly, Monday for hogs, Tuesday for calves, sheep and lambs, and Wednesday for corn, cattle, horses, sheep, hogs, lambs, poultry and butcher's meat. It had a fair annually on Midsummer's Day and two days after for horses, cattle, etc. All letters for the country as far as Norwich were put in to the *Cock and Bell* by 8 o'clock in the evening and went by mail without going to the General Post Office: the postage to London was 2d. A stage-coach set out every day from the *Lion Inn* at 9 o'clock in the morning for the *Saracen's Head*, Aldgate, or *Three Nuns*, Whitechapel, each week alternately, and returned at 3 in the afternoon: fare inside 2s. 6d., outside 1s. 3d. For goods, a stage wagon ran every Tuesday, Thursday and Saturday to the *Swan Inn*, Whitechapel, carriage 6d. per hundredweight. Some of the traders mentioned are Roger Barlow, a tailor and draper, Miss Beals, ladies boarding school, James Boram, the *Lamb Inn*, William Bourne, a carpenter, Joseph Burton, plumber and glazier, Stephen Collier and Pratt Collier were separate millers and bakers, Nathaniel Hayward an auctioneer and appraiser, William Nunn ran the *White Hart Inn* and Thomas Upwood the *Dolphin Inn*. There were four surgeons and apothecaries and three lawyers.

❧ V ❧

EVENTFUL CENTURY

At the beginning of the 19th century the famous landscape gardener Humphry Repton lived in a cottage at Hare Street, Romford. The town can claim him as a local celebrity and a green and white plaque on the wall of Lloyds Bank, which has replaced his cottage, records the fact. Repton was born at Bury St Edmunds, but moved to Norwich when he was ten. Originally trained in the calico trade, he married in 1773 and started a general merchandising business. This was not a success. Moving to Sustead, Norfolk, he made the acquaintance of William Windham of Felbrigg Hall and went to Ireland as his deputy when Windham became Secretary to the Lord Lieutenant. Returning to England in 1784, he settled down at Hare Street 'to a somewhat inelegant cottage close to a fairly busy highway'.

He soon joined the mail coach pioneer John Palmer in a scheme for safer coaches. Unfortunately he did not draw up a business agreement with Palmer for the ensuing revenue, and failed to share in the financial rewards which the Palmer family received. After the dashing of his hopes and loss of his investment, Repton spent three or four years sketching and writing at home while the new style mail coaches passed outside. He wrote a comedy, *Odd Whims*, which was not published until 1804. His major work, published in 1803, was *Observations on the Theory and Practice of Landscape Gardening*. Repton's first

commission as a landscape gardener came in 1788, from a friend of William Windham called Jeremiah Ives, on a site of 112 acres at Catton, and he must have been surprised at the way his new ideas took off with landowners.

He had found the career for which his talent fitted him. His hallmark was to produce for each commission a 'Red Book', a volume handsomely bound in red Morocco leather with gold tooling, about twelve by nine inches in size. In this he was able to use his skill as a watercolourist and writer to explain his proposals to his client. An ingenious feature was a folded flap or, in some cases, flaps which when raised showed how the scene would change on completion.

A chronicler recorded in 1832 his view of Romford's status: 'This is not a manufacturing town, nor does it possess any peculiar commercial advantages; but its extensive and well-attended market, joined to its thoroughfare situation to and from the metropolis renders its local business at all times flourishing.' The market was described as 'a very large one … held on Wednesdays; and a fair is holden on the 24th June for horned cattle and horses'. This fair is likely to have had a function as an employment exchange. Men and women would offer their services for hire to the farmers and gentry. Skilled horsemen or thatchers, or men who could perform farm

53 *The scene outside Repton's cottage at Hare Street, which he set about improving.*

54 *Repton extended his garden over the small village green, blotting out the view of the butcher's shop.*

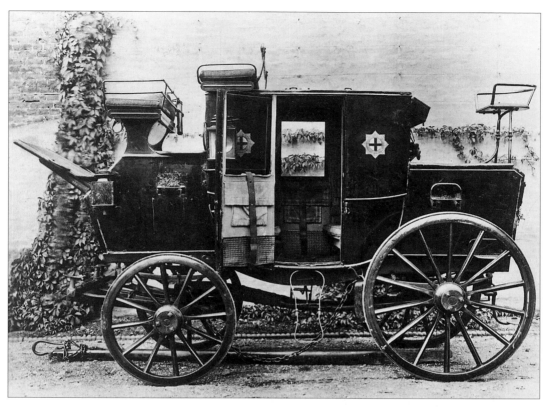

55 *The Royal Mail coach in about 1820. Seen along the Great Essex Road, this vehicle incorporated ideas for extra security devised by Palmer and Repton.*

work, were sometimes in short supply, and word of mouth often circulated the personal qualities of certain individuals better than any modern cv. One part of the local gossip network was the community of shopkeepers around the old market with its inns and taverns and the post office. From 1828 to 1833 the postmaster was Robert Surridge and the office was at his premises in the High Street. Up to 1840 it cost 4d. to post a letter to London, and unless a letter carrier was in the vicinity you had to take your letter to the post office personally. Letter boxes were only introduced in London in 1855 but by 1867 some had been installed in Romford. The post office would be a ready 'bourse' for the exchange of gossip. The post

master and his letter carriers would often transmit this onwards as they went about their business.

William Stephenson, a Romford carrier before 1840, handled distribution to all parts of London, passing through Chadwell Heath, Ilford and Stratford, starting out 'every Tuesday, Thursday and Saturday morning at Six o'Clock, and returning at midday on the same p.m.' Stephenson had taken over the business from his predecessor, Guiver. The names of a few other carriers of the early 19th century are known but there must have been many more thronging the bad roads at the time, being welcomed as a friend to the families who needed their goods delivered. Three Romford carriers

56 *Before 1847 these shops stood near the old St Edward's Church. Locals would pop in to exchange news. Built on the front of the church wall are the shambles where meat was stored between market days.*

57 *A water pump dating from the days of the horse still survives in Main Road, Gidea Park.*

of goods are listed in an 1833 directory: John Wheele's wagon, from his house in London Road, every weekday morning; Charles Halford, from his house in the High Street; and John Guiver, from his residence in North Street, every Tuesday, Thursday and Saturday. These all carried goods to London. Robert Surridge at his High Street premises, as well as having taken over as postmaster of Romford, transacted business as an agent for the Guardian Insurance Company. There were at least eight other agents, for fire and other insurance, again an index of the growing prosperity and stocks of goods and chattels in local offices, shops and homes. Many would display a 'fire-mark' on the front of the building, directing primitive fire brigades to the right house.

By 1838 a flexible system of coaches stopped at Romford so people could travel to places in Essex and beyond. One or two coaches a day went to Bury St Edmunds, Chelmsford, Colchester, Harwich and Maldon, and there was one at half past nine

58 *Carriers' wagons like this trundled the lanes of Essex delivering essential goods.*

every evening for Norwich – obviously the mail coach – stopping at the Post Office.

Their prosperity was put in jeopardy when Romford Station first appeared on the map in 1839. The railway must have caused some disturbance in the town, firstly from the gangs of navvies camped alongside the line, and then by the arrival of the snorting monster engine on the high earth bank that had been thrown across Romford, crossing the formerly quiet South Street. One effect of building the bank was to cut off the supply of wind to a mill which stood just south of the station. Romford now had a second area of activity away from the market place, the first wooden railway station of the Eastern Counties Railway being situated in Dog Lane, or Waterloo Road as it is now called. This was the site of a barracks parade ground and firing ranges dating from 1795 and an expected invasion by Napoleon. The barracks were now closed and a new area of cottage housing with spaces for small factories was built. The area also

housed many of the workers at the growing Romford Brewery, which occupied the land between Waterloo Road and South Street. At first only a limited number of passengers travelled by the seven trains which ran to and from Romford each weekday. Romford was at the end of the line while navvies were busy pushing the line on towards Brentwood and, with more difficulty, through a huge cutting to Shenfield. The departure times were 9a.m., 10.30, 12 noon, 2.30, 4, 5.30 and 7p.m.

The only other stations on the line in 1839 were Ilford, Stratford and the London terminus at Devonshire Street, Mile End. In spite of the limited service, Romford soon had its first station master, Edward Tolbutt, whose family owned land near the station.

One of Britain's oldest railway buildings stands, though somewhat altered, beside the main line at Squirrels Heath, east of Gidea Park station. There have been some alterations to convert it into housing. When

59 *On the right of this picture is the old windmill whose wind was cut off by the railway. On the left is the* Rising Sun *public house; the name was transferred to a new building, but this has now been changed to the* Goose.

the Eastern Counties Railway opened it appears there was a small locomotive depot and workshops north of the early Stratford station at Angel Lane. The locomotive depot at the country end (the railway terminated west of Barrack Lane, or Waterloo Road, Romford) was east of Whalebone Lane, Chadwell Heath, where the cutting became an embankment. Nothing now remains at this spot.

To extend the line eastwards the company had to buy the Hare Hall estate, and the company's engineer John Braithwaite actually lived in the building while the line was planned and built. There was considerable spare land south of the line, and here it was decided to build an engine house. In February 1841 the contract for the 'Engine Station at Hare Street' was awarded to a Mr Jay for £13,943. It was reported on 8 February that it would be

ready by 1 May. This seems optimistic, even considering the manpower resources available, mechanical tools and power equipment being less sophisticated at the time. In the event the roof had been put in place by October and most of the machinery had been installed but the turntable had still to arrive.

Eastern Counties Railways ran its trains on a wider gauge of five feet, which was incompatible with other early lines. Its engines, built at places like Bristol, Liverpool and Newton-le-Willows, Lancashire, had to be brought partly by sea or canal and then overland. A Mr Markwick bought four acres next to the factory in January 1843 and was contracted to build 30 cottages for company workers. By September, additional houses were ready, and the nucleus of a small railway community had been set up. The area was known as Factory Terrace, and later Factory Road. Eventually, thanks to a clergyman, a school house was created from two of the buildings. The houses have been replaced by a council housing scheme but the *New Inn* survives from this era.

The first station at Romford was on the embankment above the land between Waterloo and St Andrew's Roads. Originally the exit was via some breakneck steps on the northern side of the line. There was a public house known as the *Laurie Arms* (now demolished) at the junction of Waterloo and St Andrew's Roads, but the *Prince Albert* survives, one of the few remaining original features of the estate of working-class houses. Below the first station a small

triangular plot was used as Mr Daldy's coal depot. Above this point, in later years, cattle were off-loaded down a ramp into Waterloo Road.

A second wooden station was soon built on the bank, above the brewery site, where the Battis footpath connected South Street and Waterloo Road. Long exit slopes from this brought passengers down more conveniently into South Street. This street began to lose its rural aspect as part of the country road to Hornchurch (the stretch from the *Golden Lion* originally being called Hornchurch Lane, and the road beyond the railway arch still called Hornchurch Road into the 20th century), and began to acquire

60 *The original railway factory at Squirrels Heath.*

2. The *Caution* Signal to *Slacken Speed*, is shown by a *Green* Flag, or (in the absence of a Green Flag) by holding *One Arm Straight* up.

3. The *Danger* Signal *Always to Stop* is shown by a *Red* Flag, or (in the absence of a Red Flag) by holding *both Arms straight up*, or waving with violence a Hat or any other object.

NIGHT.

4. The Signal *All Right* is shown by a steady *White* Light.

5. The *Caution* Signal *to Slacken Speed* is shown by a steady *Green* Light.

61   *Page from a railway handbook showing signalling by the railway police.*

some smart buildings, such as the original County Court, with its Royal Arms above the entrance. The original narrow and gloomy arch over the road almost converted the town into two Romfords, people living north and south of the railway being wary of crossing the dividing line which separated them. The first station master, as we have mentioned, was a Mr Tolbutt of an old Romford family. According to Mr Springham, who remembered the early days, everything was very primitive: 'The tickets were printed on thin paper in a large book and were stamped as asked for with a hand stamp … then a knife edge was pressed on the book and the tickets torn out one by one.' Obviously, any great number of passengers would put this system under pressure. Elsewhere Mr Springham adds that the traveller's destination was written in with pen and ink on the ticket. In *White's Directory* of 1848, John Finch is the railway policeman at Romford. Dressed in elaborate uniforms of blue, at first, and later green, with tailcoats, brass buttons and top hats, his responsibility was working the points and signals as much to performing normal police work.

The second wooden version of Romford station, on its elevated bank with little protection from the wind and weather,

62   *Cartoon showing Hoy's donkey racing the train.*

must have tested the resolve of passengers proposing to travel by train. In the colder months of the year, thick clothes, and many of them, were needed.

The railway had an early reputation for unpunctuality and then the traveller boarded a far from ideal conveyance. There was quite a differentiation in first-, second- and third-class. Originally third-class carriages had no roof and second-class no windows. None of the carriages had springs. In 1848 only eight daily trains came to Romford. By 1855 this figure had increased to 18, nine for Colchester and nine for London. After the Great Eastern Railway took over in 1864, measures were taken to improve conditions, and by 1864 there were 12 local trains on the 'down' line each day. Things certainly needed to improve: on certain Eastern Counties routes trains were so slow that, in 1856, a man named George Hoy raced his 15-year-old donkey against one of the business specials and claimed later that he and his donkey conveyance had won easily. The magazine *Punch* illustrated the scene, the cartoon showing hapless third-class passengers wedged in a very basic form of commuter carriage. With due allowance for artistic licence, the conditions (third-class coaches usually having a roof by now) were those faced by many early riders behind the 'iron horse'.

The Poor Law Amendment Act of 1834 led to the building of an institution in Romford that could be called the forerunner of British welfare provision and of the National Health Service. Romford Union Workhouse was built at the far end of a large open field site in Oldchurch Road during 1838. It was meant to provide basic relief to the destitute, the old and the sick of ten parishes who had no other means of support. These folk, from Romford, Barking, Dagenham, Great Warley,

Eastern Counties' Railway.
OPEN FROM
SHOREDITCH to BRENTWOOD.

THE Public are informed that the TRAINS START from LONDON and from BRENTWOOD, calling at the intermediate Stations of Stratford, Ilford and Romford, at EVERY HOUR, from Eight o'clock in the Morning till Eight o'clock in the Evening, except at the hours of Twelve and One o'clock from London, and One and Two o'clock from Brentwood.

The Ten o'clock, Three o'clock, and Seven o'clock Trains from London, and the Ten o'clock, Twelve o'clock, Four o'clock, and Six o'clock Trains from Brentwood will not call at any of the intermediate stations.

The Five o'clock Train from London will leave first and second class passengers only at the intermediate stations without stopping.

On Sundays the Eleven o'clock and Twelve o'clock Trains do not run; but all the Trains running on Sundays take passengers to and from the intermediate stations.

Coaches are despatched daily by the Trains to Hornchurch, Upminster, Ockendon, Billericay, Rayleigh, Southend, Chelmsford, Maldon, Braintree, Halsted, Ingatestone, Witham, Colchester, Harwich, Bury, Sudbury, Ipswich, Norwich, and Yarmouth.

Omnibuses run to and from each train to the Bank, through the Strand and Piccadily, Holborn and Oxford Street, and the new road to the West-end.

Offices, High Street, Shoreditch,
July 17th, 1840.

63 *An advertisement for the extension of the railway to Brentwood in 1840 shows the printer's superior version of a railway carriage.*

Havering village, Cranham, Upminster, Hornchurch, Rainham and Wennington, were forced into the 'Union', having got into a position of absolute poverty, usually through no fault of their own, and unable to pay for food or lodging. In the harsh world of the time, thousands were struggling to survive at a basic subsistence level. A small number of charities, like Roger Reede's, were in being but generally aimed at those who had retained some respectability. The large numbers of paupers in need of medical attention were at first tended by a few staff in the sick bays of the original building.

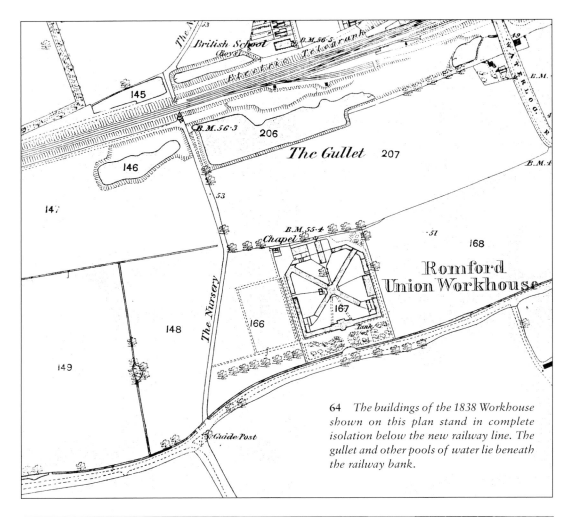

64   *The buildings of the 1838 Workhouse shown on this plan stand in complete isolation below the new railway line. The gullet and other pools of water lie beneath the railway bank.*

65   *Romford Union Workhouse Guardians and Medical and Nursing Staff pose in front of the Administrative Buildings – looking after the poor and indigent was almost an industry in itself in Victorian Romford.*

66 *Apparently rough play stopped football matches in Romford more than once. This cartoon by 'Jack B.', issued as a postcard, lampoons Romford's opponents, the Crusaders, for being too soft and the referee having to halt the match in 1906.*

67 *This late 19th-century photograph shows Romford Cricket Club members, many of whom are wearing top hats in spite of the fact that they were no longer fashionable. Fourth from left in the middle row is James Everett Dowsing, chairman of Romford Urban District Council from 1900-3.*

The original field around the workhouse was used to grow some of the inmates' food. In the early days there was also a treadmill on which the inmates worked. Superior flour was ground to raise money and sold outside, the inhabitants' meals using an inferior variety. The first separate infirmary building was constructed to the east of the

A GRAND MATCH OF CRICKET WILL BE PLAYED

AT HAVERING,

On Thursday, August 29, 1850,

BETWEEN ELEVEN OF THE

ARTIZANS

Employed at Havering,

AND ELEVEN OF THE

INHABITANTS

Of Havering.

Wickets to be pitched at 12 o'Clock Precisely. Good Accommodation on the
Ground by Mr. Osborn, Royal Oak, Havering.

HARVEY, PRINTER, BOOKBINDER, AND STATIONER, ROMFORD

68 *This interesting poster has survived of a match between workmen and local residents at Havering-atte-Bower. These men may have been unable to join the Romford Cricket Club, not being prominent local citizens.*

69 *A busy cattle market is in progress at the Laurie Hall end of the Market Place. The block of houses, part of which later became the Market Superintendent's Office, is here fully occupied and in good condition, with Davey's builders and undertakers premises at the left-hand side. Up to the First World War, this scene changed little from the mid-19th-century moment when the houses in Laurie Square at the right were built. The end one of these townhouses is seen rising above the older market building.*

original workhouse in 1893, and gradually other hospital buildings spread across the two-and-a-half-acre site. The workhouse complex almost became one of Romford's industries because of the numbers of people employed in its running and the work that was done there. In 1881, for instance, a report was published for the half year ending with Lady Day which consisted of 44 pages and listed the guardians appointed for each of the ten parishes, committees and a considerable amount of statistical information. There were no fewer than five committees, namely Assessment, School Attendance, Visiting, Finance and Removal. Two dietaries were laid out, one for able-bodied men and women and one for the infirm: so many ounces of bread and gruel or porridge for breakfast, amounts of cooked meat, potatoes and other vegetables, soup and boiled rice or suet pudding for dinner, and so much bread and cheese for supper. A list of Indoor Paupers is given and it adds up to nearly 500, almost the normal capacity of the workhouse. Outdoor Relief was given to 600 other persons in the half-year. Many widows are included. Other reasons given for the need for relief were old age or paralysis. A number of the poor applied for money to pay for a coffin to bury a member of the family.

In 1876 a young Marlborough Collegian, F.H. (later Major) Thirlwell, took up residence in Romford and founded Romford Football Club. Apparently, there was not a single club in the district at the time. The club was duly launched with a membership of about fifteen, mostly lads who had just left school. It set up its headquarters at the *White Hart Hotel* and played against other teams on the old Mawneys Ground before those fields were built over. A famous Romford sportsman, W.D. Matthews, took charge and the club began to do well, distinguishing

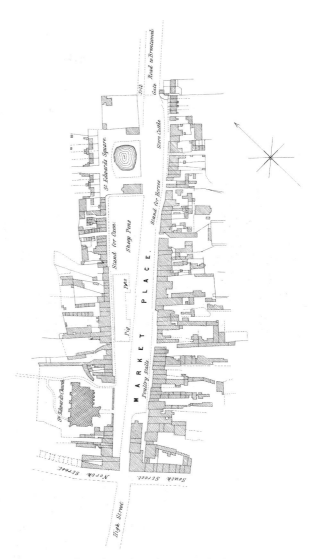

70 *A plan of Market Place, Romford, 1867.*

itself in 1881 by reaching the 5th round of the FA Cup. At this point the club was soundly thrashed by the Northern League club Darwen 15 goals to nil. The next few seasons saw the club in the doldrums. But in 1883-4, having amalgamated with local club Union FC, they again did exceptionally well in the FA Cup, before coming up against Blackburn Rovers who beat them 8-0. Rovers went on to win the first of three consecutive

71   *The Old High Street, Romford was the first area to feel the impact of the flood in 1888.*

Cup Finals. The club again went through a critical period, being saved by two of the officials who paid the annual sub to the Association. Another amalgamation, this time with a junior team called the Buffaloes, ushered in another successful era and the club was elected to the South Essex League Premier Division in 1896. One of the first county clubs to join the Essex Cup competition, it played with varying fortunes up to 1890 when defeated 2-0 by Ilford in the final. Romford reached the final in 1992-3 and 1997-8, only to succumb to Chelmsford and Leyton respectively. In 1899 it was reported that 'the South Essex League match between Leytonstone and Romford was not completed – stopped by the referee 25 minutes from time owing to a shindy on the field.'

A picture exists showing members of the Romford Cricket Club about 1850. The team was made up mostly of local traders,

clerks and businessmen. Laurie Mumford wrote a history of the club in 1963, believing that the year was their centenary. While researching this, he discovered there were records of a Romford Cricket Club playing three games in the 18th century. County newspapers could not be found mentioning their games, but *Bell's London Life and Sporting Chronicle* contained quite detailed reports on fixtures between 1847 and 1852, which suggests that Romford was already a well-known and successful club. When J.R. Clube was researching the *c.*1850 team, in which his ancestor John Clube appears, he discovered that it fielded a similar line-up against the City Club of Islington in 1849. Fashion was changing in the cricket world in about 1850 and top hats were going out and caps coming in, while braces were being replaced by belts. Bats with splices were beginning to be used. Some of the players in the 1850 Romford team, like George Mead and Thomas Bourne, had played for the Liberty Club in 1832 and 1833. A poster advertising a match between the Liberty of Havering Club and Aveley has survived.

A few warnings earlier in the 19th century had shown what might happen when the banks of the River Rom began to be hemmed in with houses. In 1841 the high water mark was about three to four feet above normal and minor damage was caused. In 1869 a local writer commented, 'This Rom is a strange romp. She runs over the banks, and with great fury makes aggressive inroads upon cellars, lower rooms and the street itself.' By 1880 the nuisance had become so great that a civil engineer was instructed by the Romford Board of Health to prepare a report. Its terms of reference were 'as to the best means of preventing the recurrence of the floods which for several years past have caused considerable damage to the properties adjoining the river Rom, and to survey the course of the river so far as it flows through the district of the Board and advise as to the causes of the floods and as to what is necessary or can be done to lessen the evil'. In the report, submitted in March 1881, the engineers recommended the diversion of some of the streams emptying into the Rom north of the High Street bridge. They commented on the increased drainage of streams from a wide area into this part of the Rom which had formerly flowed into other courses southwards. Several other suggestions were made and some of the works were carried out soon afterwards, but they may not have been completed seven years later, when Romford was hit by its greatest flood.

The events of August 1888 exceeded all previous experiences in Romford. Heavy rains had fallen for a fortnight and reached a climax on the night of 1 and 2 August, when there was a particularly violent thunderstorm. While the town was sleeping, the River Rom overflowed, the culvert under the High Street bridge and in the way of the seething onslaught failing to carry it. Thousands of tons of water crested straight over the top of the parapet, taking all before it, including the massive brewery entrance gates. Thirty thousand beer barrels were washed away from the extensive brewery grounds, past Oldchurch, towards Dagenham and the Thames beyond. It is recorded that in southern parts of the district, at South Hornchurch, Dagenham and in the other scattered hamlets, crowds

72 *The railway line was also submerged and the water so deep that it put out fires in the engines, bringing traffic to a complete halt.*

73 *Scene at the back of the brewery after the flood. Brewery staff and others stand amazed at the scale of the damage. It is recorded that there was three feet of water at the highest point in their yard, and one reporter commented, 'The storage chambers were completely submerged and an immense amount of damage was done. Passing from the High Street, the water rushed like a torrent through the brewers' yard, tearing up pavements, overthrowing brick walls and bursting the end wall, about 50 foot long, of a two-storied building. Such a wreck at the brewery was never known and the loss to the firm is colossal.'*

of onlookers 'rescued' floating barrels that were full of beer, breaking them open with any implement to hand and consuming the contents. Production on farms, factories and elsewhere must have taken a steep drop for a few days! Water filled Romford High Street several feet deep, ruining the stock of many shopkeepers, who crowded into what was then the principal trading street. Horses, some of them up to their necks in water, were rescued and ridden out of the Angel Yard and other High Street passages.

Early on Wednesday mornings it was a common sight to see cattle and sheep being driven along the roads leading to the market, the drovers hollering as they brandished their long sticks. Carts and wagons would follow, bringing goats, pigs, poultry and other farm products. After the market was set up, horse-drawn vehicles of every description would carry in people and farm folk from all around. Theresa Bibbings remembered that the main business of the market did not start till after 12 o'clock, by which time it was very crowded and noisy and smelt like a farmyard. The centre was a confusion of horses and carts and the scales were at the north end (near the Laurie Hall). Cows were tethered to the rail along the west side and were milked where they stood. Between the cows and the centre were sheep and pig pens, and tethered goats, and south of these were farm implements, tools, scrap iron, Wellington boots etc. spread over the cobbles. Here cheapjacks took their stand. Horses and donkeys were tethered to the rail on the (south-) east side, which stretched from the school to Mr Stone's small draper's shop.

At this time South Street was a quiet shopping centre, graced by the trees in Dr Wright's garden. People rarely visited doctors as they charged 2s. 6d., but Mr Bray the chemist in the High Street would prescribe

74 *One local store rebuilt its premises at the key business location on the corner of High Street and South Street. At the beginning of 1882, J.W. Lasham had been running a successful business as chemist and druggist for many years and wished to consolidate with a new landmark building. He had been using a partial conversion of a very old public house called the* Crown, *dating back to the 15th or 16th century. When this was demolished it was discovered that it had been constructed on a very substantial oak framework and a description was given in* The Building News *for 27 January 1882: 'the spaces between the timbers being filled in flush, both sides, with a composition of well-beaten clay, straw, and chalk, which had become almost as hard as stone. Imbedded in this were stout oak laths, held in position by cross sticks, to which they were bound by hazel withies; no nail being used in any part of the work. This construction is not uncommon in the county, and is wonderfully durable. The new premises comprise warehouses and extensive cellarage in the basement; a shop on the ground-floor, at the corner; and a spacious residence on the upper floors for the proprietor; several sets of offices on the ground and first floors; with separate entrance in South Street and two small shops. Thus the whole of the street frontage on the ground floor is utilised for business purposes. The walls are built of brick and where exposed externally are faced with red bricks; the pilasters and entablature of the shop fronts are of Portland Stone.' The younger Lasham had taken over from his father earlier in the 19th century, and among his staff in the new building was a young man who would make a big impact on the town, namely Tommy England. He would take over the business when Lasham junior retired.*

75   *Building the new copper at Ind Coope's Romford brewery in the late 19th century. The several gentlemen involved stand or, in one case, sit proudly in front of the construction. At the front of the group on the left, from the left, are: Mr Lovell, A. Martin, Mr Beamish and Mr Loder. On the right are E.S. Palmer, Mr Richardson (seated), Thomas Bird and Hammond. The brewery had developed from a successful public house (The Star) in existence at the end of the 18th century. The slightly ramshackle nature of the operations, where new machinery was fitted in to the older structures for decade after decade, can be clearly seen. In January 1909, according to the Cornell Manuscript, a crisis was reached in the affairs of the brewery, a receiver being appointed by the High Courts to manage the businesses in Romford and at Burton. According to Cornell, the reason for the troubles were the many changes made in the staff and management, old and tried servants being dismissed to make way for less competent men. The brewery survived until the late 20th century when, having become part of a multi-national, it was ruthlessly swept away and sold off. The money spent on new buildings and infrastructure in the modern era was forfeit on the whim of a faceless consortium.*

76   *An informal snap of the opening of Gidea Park Garden Suburb on 1 June 1911. While the spectators sit on the grass or on fold-up chairs under a huge tree, the presentation party conduct proceedings on a temporary platform. Here the first prize is presented to the winning architect.*

77   *John Burns MP, President of the Local Government Board, with some of the workmen who built the estate.*

78   *A corner of Meadway in the early days of the estate. On the reverse of the photograph is the comment 'Price of houses £500 each.'*

79   *More of the unique architect-designed houses look freshly completed in this photograph. A brochure quotes, 'For the benefit of plot purchasers on the estate a novel system of plot purchase by instalments combined with life assurance has been arranged, and by the extension of the same system, anyone building a house on the estate can obtain the bulk of the money necessary for building, on mortgage repayable by instalments over a term of from fifteen to twenty years.'*

80 *A traffic-free South Street in about 1911. Note the narrowness of this top end. The Picture Pavilion cinema competed with the Laurie in the Market Place. This right-hand side was demolished after 1930, leading to a considerable widening.*

81 *One of the first motor cabs at Romford Station, seen next to a horse-drawn vehicle.*

82 *Motor vehicles are beginning to appear in the High Street in about 1921. On the left, an upper storey is lettered with the sign 'Motors', but there were probably still more horse-drawn vehicles on the road at this time than there were motor cars.*

for all minor ailments at no cost except for the medicine. North Street, beyond the first quarter of a mile, was bordered by farms and the parks of the gentry, such as the Marshalls Estate.

But things were about to change, as Victoria's reign finished and Edward VII's began. New shops were built on the open ground of the old White Hart Hoppet in South Street and in the High Street facing up Mawney Road. Food began to be packaged in tins and cardboard cartons, or paper wrappers, and branded with the name of the producer. Previously many food items had been put in a brown paper bag straight from the barrel or marble slab. Chain shops began to supplant some of the local businesses, starting the trend which now means that town centres everywhere contain the same 'multiples'.

In the first decade of the 20th century, the area known as Hare Street and the grounds of Gidea Hall were chosen to be the site of an experimental Garden Suburb. Still unique in its way, and known by architects worldwide, the Suburb has to a certain ex-

tent blended into the later development. Its unique nature is partly a factor of the advanced ideas shared by some architects and town planners at the time of its birth and partly due to its being tucked away between a public park, Raphael Park, and a golf course. The houses display features of the Arts and Crafts movement and the ideas of William Morris. The company which created this enclave was floated by three Liberal MPs, but particularly by Herbert Henry Raphael, who had purchased the former estate of Gidea Hall, started the Golf Club, and donated a substantial area of land to the townspeople of Romford. The scheme originated as an architectural competition and many famous architects contributed designs for well-built houses which were meant to raise the standard of building in the country as a whole. Although intended for the average person, the houses were so successful that the estate became a most superior one and the houses much sought after.

Edward Fisk remembered that the roads in Romford at the beginning of the 20th century 'were bad, being narrow and

83 *One of Ind Coope brewery's motor vehicles, used as a fire engine to deal with outbreaks on the premises, is now housed in a museum.*

made with gravel or grit, hardened by steam roller. Some were not paved but the market square was cobbled'. John Hewitt remembered 'when Mawney Road was being done up beyond the *Mawney Arms* in 1902 or thereabouts. They filled in the pot-holes here and there and sprinkled sand all over, watering it with the water cart, then along came a steam roller to roll it all in. But a steam roller was one of those dangerous power-driven vehicles, so it arrived with a man walking in front with a red flag. Romford in 1908-10 had no buses and, of course, very little traffic. In the evenings after the shops had shut South Street was practically empty and people out for the evening strolled down the middle of the road. Going through on a push-cycle, one rang the bell almost continuously and rode in and out of the people in zig-zag fashion.' A prominent shopkeeper in South Street, Mr Muskett, was killed about this time in a collision with a bicycle.

Cars began to appear in very small numbers, putting new hazards on the narrow streets. John Hewitt's first ride was at the General Election in 1906, with a short trip along part of South Street in a French manufactured Darracq. On

7 May 1906 a Council Minute expressed the view that 'serious attention should be drawn to the terrible nuisance and damage caused by motor vehicles in this District ... serious danger accrues to persons using the highways from the motor vehicles raising great clouds of dust as to render the sight of other vehicles almost impossible to give time to get out of the way.' As late as 8 April 1913 the council received a letter from Mr H.W. Palmer complaining of the use of Eastern Road from the Garage in South Street for motor trials, and of the noise thereby created; the recommended action was for the Clerk of the Council to communicate with the police about the matter.

Many of the first owners of motor cars were doctors. A new doctor setting up his practice in Romford, Dr Harold Upward, at first visited patients on a bicycle, not being able to afford a horse and carriage. When he was better established, he acquired a one-cylinder De Dion Bouton motor car, and a chauffeur, Frederick Harold, who attended it with loving care. With the advent of the First World War, Upward joined the Royal Army Medical Corps on active service. The De Dion had to be sold and Frederick got a job at Romford brewery.

VI

IN THE LINE OF DUTY

The war opened with much jingoism but also plenty of chaos. Romford and Hornchurch men who volunteered to join up, locally or in London, were often dispatched to training camps in other parts of the country. Conversely, other potential soldiers from all over Britain found themselves billeted in local schools and camps in Romford and Hornchurch.

All the time there was a need to house the growing numbers of volunteers in training. Many soldiers found themselves in very spartan conditions, one area that came into use in 1915 being the house and grounds of Hare Hall. Over the fields of the estate stretching from Brentwood Road to Main Road, a competent group built superior huts for what was to be the Artists' Rifles

84 *This view of the sleepy Hare Street district, taken from the middle of the Main Road, shows how rural the scene was in 1908. In fact, the Premier Coffee House, in an old cottage on the left, with its rather ramshackle extension towards the road, was almost certainly opened to serve the needs of cyclists and walkers on recreational trips, rather than for the convenience of locals. But everything was about to change. Within a year or two the Gidea Park Garden Suburb would be built just around the corner, and soon a bus service from the East End would terminate at the* Unicorn *public house seen in the right distance. After the First World War broke out, large numbers of soldiers in training would be using the cafes and shops which had sprung up to serve the new community based at Hare Hall camp.*

85   *Hare Hall camp was superbly organised, as this view of an athletics event on 8 August 1917 shows. The runners bear the initial letter of their teams. The spectators include the Artists Rifles as well as many local ladies and gentlemen. Life for the soldiers would be different once they had been dispatched to the conflict on the front line in France.*

86   *A proud soldier poses with his lady in a garden. Note the puttees, a particularly irksome part of First World War uniform.*

87   *Friendships were struck up in the camp, creating a comradeship that would be remembered by the officer when sent to the horrors overseas.*

88   *A view of well-built huts against a background of the tall trees that ringed the Hare Hall estate, a tranquil piece of the England for which the Artists Rifles would be fighting.*

89   *Local ladies formed soccer teams while their boys were fighting in France. Most were at work in factories, large and small, connected with the war in some way. These came from Brock's blouse factory, which in 1916 was hard at work in North Street opposite the old Labour Exchange, possibly producing clothing for the women's forces.*

90   *A group of officers by the steps of Gidea Hall, another mansion pressed into service by the Artists Rifles training battalion.*

91   *A sketch drawn in the autograph book of a nurse at the military hospital by one of the wounded soldiers. A soldier replies satirically to a foolish questioner, a rather frequent occurrence. The soldier is clearly wearing the uniform sported by wounded soldiers recuperating in a military hospital.*

92   A large group comprising wounded soldiers, nurses, helpers and officers in charge sit for their photograph
at Marshalls, an overflow centre for the wounded. As the soldier comments to his fiancée, 'Hospital would
have been perhaps better but Marshalls is sufficient.' There were fewer facilities for treatment here than at
the main hospital at Oldchurch. Everybody in the picture is trying to put a brave face on things, 'in spite
of the times we live in', as the writer puts it.

93   A drumhead
service by the War
Memorial for the fallen
of the First World
War. The provision
of a War Memorial
and the form it should
take was the subject
of special meetings of
the Romford Urban
District Council from
1919. This 'cenotaph'
was eventually built,
but other suggestions
included the creation
of a playing field
somewhere off the
London Road with a
monument placed on it.
Also discussed was the
erection of a YMCA
centre, which would
benefit the young by
providing facilities edu-
cational and otherwise,
especially appropriate
given the service
provided to men in
France and local camps
by that organisation.

94   *The War Memorial which once stood in Laurie Square, the site of the present Ludwigshafen Place and underpass, was removed when the latter was constructed to the old burial ground in Main Road. This photograph shows it after the annual Commemoration of Remembrance service in 2001.*

training camp, through which thousands of more skilled volunteers from civilian life would be trained to become officers.

Entertainment was available to both locals and the encamped soldiers in the town. Cinema shows of a primitive kind were available at the Picture Pavilion in South Street and at the Laurie Cinema in a converted Victorian building at the top end of the Market Place. All films were silent, but a pianist seated at the front of the auditorium followed what was happening on the screen with an appropriate melody. Some of the pianists were ladies. At this time there were few proper bathrooms in houses, and the personal hygiene of many in the audience was questionable, so between performances attendants would go round the auditorium with disinfectant from a basic spray gun.

Local ladies also formed groups to knit items of useful clothing for the men on the front line in France and Belgium. Others were involved in various nursing organisations, some even going to the front as medical auxiliaries and accompanying wounded soldiers back to Britain for treatment. As the war progressed a military hospital was set up in Oldchurch Workhouse Infirmary, where large numbers of the wounded were treated. There were also overflow centres, at, for instance, Marshalls mansion.

VII

THE GOLDEN MILE AND CIVIC PRIDE

After the First World War tremendous changes in retailing took place. Romford gradually acquired the status of a premier shopping centre, and as each year passed new shops opened and more branded goods and chain stores appeared in the town. In the inter-war period, few families possessed a car, but in the Romford area the proportion of car owners was higher than the average in Britain. But the key to Romford's shopping development was the large number of bus services running through the town to other parts. Romford was widely known as a place for a 'day out', especially on cattle market day (Wednesday). A Chamber of Commerce was set up in 1919 and there is no doubt that businesses had a strong influence on the way the town developed.

95 *This picture of Oliver and Ethel Fawkes outside their shop shows what were quite old-fashioned display methods by the 1930s. Though they appear well-established here at number 88, their only reference in local directories places them at 64 North Street in 1933, and in the 1937 edition of* Kelly's *the shop is at 52 North Street. On both occasions their telephone number was Romford 1048.*

96   *London General buses in the Market Place.*
The proprietors LGOC were bringing increasing
numbers of people to Romford in the 1920s.
In this picture are open-top and covered buses.
The market was now less agricultural and
aimed more at locals and visitors. The fruit and
vegetable and sweet and confectionery stalls, and
hawkers selling patent medicines, were among
those attending. At the same time, the livestock
market was reaching the peak of its importance
before decline set in after 1936. The expansion
of the market continued even as new multiple
shops were coming into the town.

97   *Wireless advertising in the 1930s. High*
fidelity it is not!

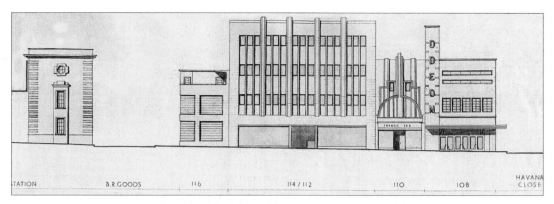

98 *Panorama of South Street drawn in 1954 but showing the Golden Mile of shopping and entertainment at its height in the 1930s. Because of the shortage of materials and priority given to repairing wartime damage, little had changed. So this is a view of one side of possibly the most successful 1930s shopping street in the London suburbs. The section begins with the Station House, rebuilt together with the bridge over South Street in 1930 when, in a major railway widening project, four tracks replaced the original two. Then we have the open space, where a refreshment stall was sometimes parked at night, leading into the Battis footpath, followed by the cinema block. On the left corner is the modernistic replacement of the old Star pub by an American bar, then the Times Furnishing Company, then Frances Dee, ladies fashions, then the cinema. As a record of the street at this time, the drawing is only marred by the spelling 'Francis Dee'.*

Fawkes and White (Illustration 95) was not the only small business in Romford in the inter-war period. In the 1920s a promotional booklet called *The Home Seekers' Guide to Romford* advertised the following:

Lasham's the cash chemist. The corner of South and High Streets – all wireless requisites stocked – listening in by appointment – goods not in stock procured the same day – photographic films developed daily – Marcel Waving and manicures – Vibro Massage by skilled Lady Manageress. Branch at 35 Victoria Road.

Meadmore's Licensed Restaurant – high class cakes and confectionery – deliveries by motor daily – agent for all wines and bottled beers (14 High Street). John T. King – Footwear and foot-trouble specialist – for Golf Shoes of merit – 'K' Agency – the finest selection in the County of High-class Walking and Shooting Boots – Hand-sewn Boots made to measure and High-class Repairs – Chiropodist. (72a South Street).

Daldy and Co. (G.F. Daldy) – Coal and English Timber Merchants – Best House and Steam Coals (including Anthracites) of all descriptions, and Coke always in stock – Truck Loads sent to any Railway Station – Contractors for Oak, Chestnut & Fir Fencing (93 South Street).

W. Wackett – Cheapest Yard for all kinds of New and Second-hand Building Material, Wire Netting, Chestnut Fencing, Doors, Window Sashes, Stoves, Guttering, Paints, Nails, Tar, Creosote, Ruberoid and Sanded Felts – All kinds of fittings and everything in the building trade at lowest prices. 100 Tons of Firewood always in stock. – Buildings bought for demolition (Hill House, Market Place).

M. Masel – We are proud to be known in the District as the Cheapest and best shop for: Electric, Gas, Oil. – Heating and Lighting Appliances. – All household goods, Paints, Wallpapers, Distemper, etc. – Soaps, polishes, brushes, brooms, etc. – Garden Tools, Wire Netting, Fretwork Tools – Materials, Designs. – Wireless Sets, parts and materials. – Lowest

99   *An oblique view of the Havana Cinema block at its inception. The cinema name was changed in 1949 to the Odeon. Belying its narrow frontage, it provided 2,500 seats in the auditorium across the back of the block.*

100   *The same view seen in about 1905 from the railway bridge.*

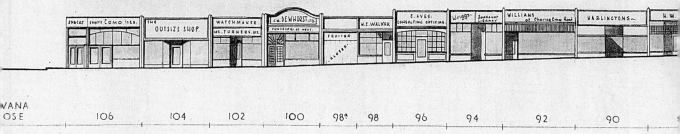

101 *The one-storey block of shops that was still surviving in 1954 housed ten businesses, only a couple of which were part of larger concerns, with other branches. The Como Café later transferred into premises on the other side of the railway bridge across the road, occupying the old separate booking hall of the Upminster Railway. This building originally had a mini-balustrade running along the tops of the façade. Another mis-spelling of a shop, occurring fourth from right, is Wings, 'Bookshop and Library'. H.W. Hole served as a councillor and was Chairman of the Urban District Council, and illustrates the part played by local businessmen in directing the affairs of the town between the wars.*

Prices, Highest Quality, Delivered Free anywhere.

Frostick and Sons – The original practical chimney cleaners, carpet beaters – Carpets taken up and relaid if required. Frostick and sons beg to tender their most sincere thanks for the kind support they have received for the past 40 years, and hope, by their strict attention to all orders, combined with good workmanship and civility to still retain the kind support of the inhabitants of Romford and surrounding district. Also beg to inform the public that this business has not been sold, but is still carried on at the same address. Should you require any of the above work executed, kindly make arrangements with bearer, by post or call at the above address and oblige,

Your obedient servants
Frostick & Sons

No connection with Frostick Bros. (members of the same family had set up a rival business and were hoping to trade on the good name of the original firm).

G. Ives – Mercury Nurseries – Garden Contractor – Choice supplies of fruit trees, shrubs, roses, bulbs etc. – Also large stock of perennials and summer bedding plants – Church Decorations for Weddings, Concerts, etc. – Advice and estimates free at any time (established 1823). Contractor to H.M. Government, Stand in Market, Wednesdays and Saturdays (in the Upper Market Place, entrance to which was along a delightful footpath behind the St Edward's School building leading to the nursery, the original Mercury Gardens, which ran through to Western Road, the end gate being closed once a year to establish trader's right of ownership. The concrete canyon of the present Mercury Gardens, many times the width, is a far cry from the original.)

Poel Brothers (J.B. Poel) – Horse Motor and Steam Cartage and Haulage Contractors – Clinker, Sand, Ballast, Hogging, Hardcore, etc. supplied – Ice Merchants – All the year round daily deliveries from the Romford Ice Factory (North Street, Romford and Church Lane).

T.F. Collett's Fruit Store – Canned Fruit, Fresh Fruit, Vegetables – The best obtainable salads fresh daily – Vegetables from the leading local growers – cleanliness – quality – freshness. Free delivery to all parts of Romford – the Golden Rule of Health: EAT MORE FRUIT.

Richard Banyard, Nelmes Farm – Producer of Pure Milk. Will supply you with the Purest and Very Best Milk, Cream, Butter and Eggs twice daily from the choicest

102 *H.W. Hole's advert in a local publication of 1938. He provided the kind of services which brought people to Romford.*

herd of cows. The delivery Depots are – 19 North Street and 64 Victoria Road, Romford. For Invalids and Nursery Purposes this Milk cannot be beaten. – Inspection at all times invited.

The early days of radio, then known as wireless, in the 1920s were spent trying to hold a crystal 'cat's whisker' in position so

as to receive the transmissions, which at first were broadcast for only a few hours a day. Just walking across the room could make the whisker jump and the sound would be lost. Later, wireless sets were made with permanent reception which ran off a heavy battery called the accumulator, which was filled with acid. This had to be taken to a garage or some other depot to be recharged or exchanged and carried carefully so the acid would not spill onto clothes. That chore would be left until pay day when there was money available.

In Romford there were a number of radio dealers from the 1920s onwards, and the different models which were updated each year were widely advertised. There were scores of British manufacturers, including Ecko, Pye, Ferguson, Lissen, Brownie and Celestion. The *Radio Times* started to become a bestseller, and there was also the weekly *Popular Wireless*, required reading for the more technical enthusiasts. A knowledge of early wireless technology was put to good use when the next war came. One of

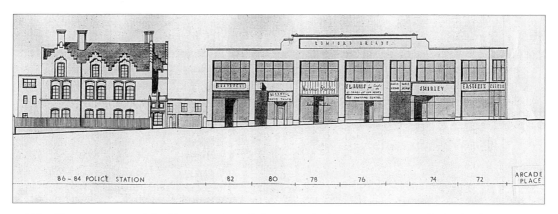

103 *The next range of buildings northwards began with the Police Station, which also housed the Magistrates Court. Stanley Manning says the Police Station front office was approached by a downward incline. It was a large rambling building, erected in 1892 and in use until December 1965. The next block was built as the Romford Arcade in 1930 and brought an early example of undercover shopping to the street. The entranceway between Flaum's and Shirley's (two clothes shops) led into a small interior passage with a few businesses leading off, such as Eagle Surgical (selling trusses and other surgical appliances), Jays Arcade Library and Romford Amusement Arcade.*

104   *Before South Street became less residential, these grand houses stood on what was to become at the end of the 19th century the Romford Arcade site.*

Romford's main radio stores was Silcocks of 55-8 High Street and later 20 South Street. In the 1930s they began to sell a few television sets, which initially had tiny screens fitted in large consoles, to wealthier residents. Smarts, at 2a/2b Quadrant Arcade, promoted Ultra's radio sets, the best value for money in 1937. Miss P. Corbell recalls listening at that time: 'Some of my earliest memories are of listening to Band Wagon, with Arthur Askey and 'Stinker' Murdoch living in an imaginary flat above Broadcasting House. In Children's Hour, Uncle Mac and Romany (the presenters) took us on lovely country walks.'

The Barclay's end of the line of shops was erected in about 1902 on an open plot known as the White Hart Hoppet (a field behind the public house in the High Street) and a wonderful view of dozens of buildings of all shapes and sizes in Ind

105   *Craddocks was a very popular shop, patronised by locals and visitors for all kinds of stationery as well as Christmas cards and presents.*

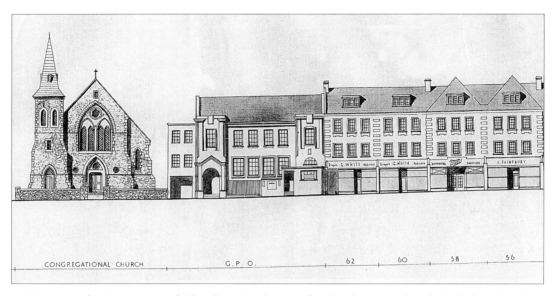

106   *From the Congregational Church to Sainsbury's. The church was a relic of the 19th- and early 20th-century period when South Street contained mainly small shops or large houses and gardens, many of them owned by doctors. It provided a meeting place, especially for newcomers to Romford. Behind it the church hall, known as the Carlisle Institute, was the scene of concerts and other social occasions.*

107   *You've got mail! Two postmen trundle sacks of mail down the middle of South Street, with the Post Office on the left. Beyond the Post Office and behind the trees are the front gardens of Dr Alfred Wright's house and a house at one time used as a boys' school. On the right, before the row of shops, trees front a garden and open space used in about 1917 to house German prisoners of war.*

108   *Looking up from Western Road corner, on the right, we see the church, Post Office and line of shops on the left-hand side. On the right are the single-storey shops with the balustrade above leading to the new Plaza cinema, opened on 20 January 1930, built to a high standard and approached up a long walkway. Today the entrance to the Mall shopping centre is on this spot. Beyond, the street has not yet been widened, and the wooden cladding on the side of the end house, which will soon be pulled down together with the buildings beyond it in order to widen the street, carries advertisements. In the panorama opposite, White's Drapers and Milliners continued to trade until the late 20th century. It once had an overhead vacuum system which ferried money and change to each counter from a central cashier's office. Sainsbury's, on the end, had moved down the street, originally being next to Barclay's Bank. It was possible up to the '60s to get off a bus here, shop in White's, Boot's and Sainsbury's, cross the road to Marks and Spencer on the rebuilt east side, and catch a bus again within about 25 minutes.*

Coope's brewery could be had. Williamson's was a superior tearoom, long and narrow with three rows of tables, starched white linen and glittering cutlery. Patrons were served by smartly dressed waitresses. It was the highlight of a visit to Romford shops and market for many.

On 16 September 1937 Romford was elevated from the status of an urban district to that of a borough. As it was coronation year for King George VI, who had approved the grant of a charter to the town, it was not possible to send a member of the Royal Family, who were all busy, so instead the Lord Mayor of London was selected to perform the handing over. In his speech he made the following point: 'In undertaking this duty I remember with interest that two former Lord Mayors of London were citizens of Romford, namely Sir Thomas Cooke of Gidea Hall, who was Lord Mayor in the year 1642-3, and Sir John Eyles, Lord Mayor in the year 1688, and it is with real pleasure that I renew these associations. Furthermore London today has close ties with the new Borough through a large residential population having business interests in the City, but although modern development has resulted in this additional link, it is pleasing to know that Romford

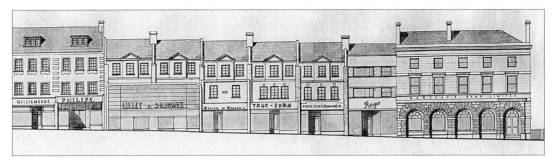

109   *Continuation of the perspective drawing of the west side of South Street from Williamson's Cafe to Barclays Bank.*

still retains much of its original character as a self-contained township, and still remembers with pride its long and noble history so intimately connected, through the Royal Palaces formerly standing in its constituent village of Havering-atte-Bower, with the Kings and Queens of England.'

Achieving the status of borough had been worked on for a number of years. The administrators of the former urban district had to prove their worthiness in municipal governance in various areas. They were helped by the achievements and professionalism of certain borough officers in planning new housing schemes and a high standard of street lighting. The government inspection team looking at Romford's application must have sometimes wavered over their decision, for it had taken the Rotary Club to prod the urban

110   *An Edwardian scene in South Street, with several horse-drawn vehicles and a cyclist. The trees on the left are in front of two former houses, and on the right are the very old-fashioned buildings which were converted into shops but demolished in the 1930s. South Street was very narrow in the early 1900s.*

111   *The top end of the panorama shows three smart shops and the bank as they were in about 1912. Lush and Cook, the cleaners, were a national firm. The frontage is full of lettering proclaiming the various services offered, including 'Cricketing Flannels cleaned in a few days'. Next door is Boot's original shop, and beyond that Sainsbury's. In spite of this aggregation of large retailers, the small-scale local shop was still very important up to 1939 and beyond. In 1937, over 86 per cent of retail firms were non-multiples. However, the trend was for change, and the widening of South Street resulted in higher rents, eventually pricing out the small concerns.*

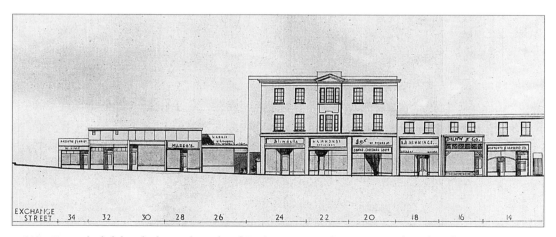

112   *From the left hand edge to the right of Exchange Street the streetscape has altered since the 1930s, bombing in the Second World War leading to a row of temporarily premises. In the 1930s a run of pretty ancient buildings, originally houses converted into shops, stood here quite unaffected by modernisation elsewhere. They can be seen in background of the above photograph. Sims the florist also had a shop in the Quadrant Arcade on the opposite side of the street. The arcade linking South Street and the Market Place added to South Street's shopping attractions.*

113 *This wartime picture shows the devastation behind shops demolished on 15 December 1940 when the Telephone Exchange was also badly damaged. The view from White Hart Yard shows part of the Quadrant Arcade frontage behind the damaged area.*

district into providing a library building which Essex County Council could then maintain. There was no municipal theatre but there were recreation grounds and a serviceable if ageing swimming bath. The key to success was the tremendous vitality of the shopping centre and the exceptional growth in population.

The growth in housing in the inter-war period was phenomenal. Not all of it was as well built as it should have been, but generally speaking it was above average. A particularly interesting development was at the Gidea Park Garden Suburb. A second exhibition was instituted to provide up-to-date dwellings on the edge of the original suburb, Eastern Avenue having been opened in 1925. This contemporary development provided a backdrop for the Gidea Park

Modern Homes Exhibition of 1934, and there were also pieces of land south of this where houses could be built in line with the latest trends. This resulted in a number of flat-roofed dwellings similar to those being built on the continent. These can still be seen today although some have altered roofs.

Although new houses appeared in all parts of Romford, many towards the outer boundaries of the district, North Romford and Collier Row were particular hotspots. A commentator of the time wrote, 'The old order changeth giving place to the new, and we give here details of the Romford that is still being developed. Take Rise Park Estate, some 1,500 houses will be erected there, while Mr T.F. Nash proposes to erect some 1,000 houses. Other estates will also

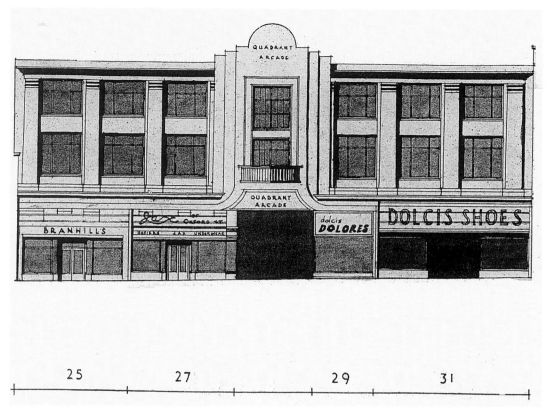

114 *A drawing of the Quadrant Arcade elevation in 1954. This was the first part of the project to be opened, and included the Dolcis shop and the Dance Hall upstairs. Started in February 1934, the work at the Market Place end was finally completed and the whole development opened at 2.30 p.m. on Monday, 23 September 1935. W. Goodchild, the promoter, dreamed up the project while recovering from an operation for appendicitis in the Victoria Cottage Hospital, Romford.*

add their quota, so that in less than five years from now we can expect the borough to grow to over double the size it is today with a population of possibly 140,000.' This statement was made in 1937, when only two years remained before the outbreak of war. The Lodge Farm Estate is described as being developed by Seymour Estates Ltd. 'This estate lies between the old market town of Romford and its modern suburb Gidea Park. A number of attractive types of house are being developed throughout the estate, all of modern design and at prices to suit every intended purchaser. All prices include

legal charges and mortgage costs. Weekly repayments for every £100 borrowed mount to only 3 shillings per week over a period of twenty years.'

On the western border was the Seabrook Estate, Crow Lane, built by Wood and Wren. A description said that it 'is well situated occupying a very accessible position in Crow Lane, adjoining the London and North Eastern Railway, within a few minutes walk of the proposed "Crowlands station". The main London Road with its excellent service of Buses and Green Line Coaches is within five minutes walk, and schools, shops

115 *The last section brings us to the top of South Street on the west side. The small but imposing classical-style Westminster Bank building was vacated in 1964, the staff operating temporarily from a building at the far end of the Market Place. It has been said that the building was so solid it took a lot of demolishing. A revolutionary new structure with a first-floor banking hall accessed by escalator has since come and gone. Green's Stores, opened in Romford during the First World War, was part of an extensive chain, one of several other local branches being situated at Hare Street, Gidea Park. Paige, part of a national chain of ladies dress shops, was one of a dozen womenswear outlets in South Street. Finally, the Fifty Shilling Tailors opened in July 1939 just before war was declared. Its full plate-glass windows represented the height of '30s style, with silver lettering on a black fascia and the Georgian-style upper floors containing office space for insurance firms and similar financial businesses.*

116 *Looking down from the top end of South Street in about 1908, we see Westgate and Hammond's shop already occupying a similar position to that of 1954, a comment on the success of the professional sector in Romford.*

117   A 1930s photograph of the top corner of South Street, showing the Lasham's building of 1882 *just before it was replaced by the Fifty Shilling Tailors.*

118   *Taken from above Lloyds Bank, this photograph shows the Lord Mayor of London's procession turning the corner into South Street on their way to the Havana Cinema for the Charter Ceremony. The Lord Mayor had halted in the Market Place just before this and addressed a gathering of thousands of local schoolchildren from a dais outside St Edward's Church.*

119 *Romford Town Hall in the 1960s. The opening of this building was performed by the Lord Mayor Sir George Broadbridge, KCVO. He had been driven to Gallows Corner and welcomed by the High Sheriff of Essex and the Charter Mayor, Councillor Charles Allen. The route along tree-lined Main Road had obviously been carefully chosen as the most attractive processional route into the town. At the Town Hall the Lord Mayor had been introduced to prominent local people, including Mr John Parker, MP for Romford, Alderman H. de Havilland, Chairman of Essex County Council, and also Captain F.R. Peel, Chief Constable of Essex. Councillor W.M. Goldsmith, Vice Chairman of the Urban District Council, formally presented Sir George with a golden key, with which he opened the door of the new Town Hall while flags above the building were simultaneously unfurled. Inside the Lord Mayor unveiled a plaque commemorating the occasion.*

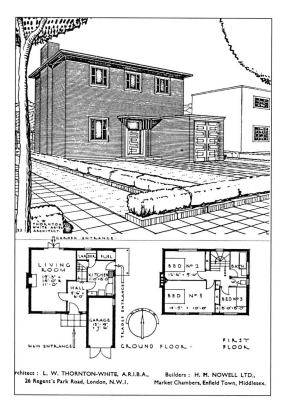

120 *A Class C dwelling in the Modern Homes Exhibition.*

121 *New houses in Clockhouse Lane, Collier Row in the 1930s. The house on the right has the rounded windows much favoured by the house builder Nash.*

122   *These 'ladies' seem to be having lots of fun as they wait by their float to take part in a 1930s Romford Carnival procession.*

and churches are all within easy reach.' Unfortunately for the would-be purchaser, Crowlands Station never came into being, although preliminary work for the platforms was undertaken. However, the Green Line coaches were at 15-minute intervals and ran an express service with only selected stops to Aldgate.

House building on the Park View Estate in Gidea Park was described as follows: 'Mr Walter White of Colwyn, Links Avenue, Gidea Park, who has been for many years building in Romford, is now developing this Estate. The houses are all semi-detached or detached and well spaced, a number of varying types being intermingled to give a most pleasing aspect to the roads. The estate is adjoining Raphael Park and Eastern Avenue and there is a wide Boulevard with lawns and ornamental trees and shrubs forming the entrance to the estate, while all the other roads on the estate are lined with trees and shrubs. The prices of the houses and bungalows varies from £815 to £905 freehold and includes such types as the modern sun-trap with curved glass windows and metal casements, while on the other hand there is a popular design of Tudor elevation incorporating herringbone brickwork and Oak timbering.'

VIII

WAR COMES HOME

123 *Training of personnel started before war began and various air-raid precautions booklets and manuals were issued to cope with expected situations. These air-raid wardens are practising moving injured people in hazardous situations. During the 'phoney war', personnel were actually given many more months to improve their performance.*

Romford began to prepare for war as it became increasingly likely from the mid-1930s onwards. Three particular worries concerned government officials: the need to protect civilians against aerial attack – the example of the Spanish Civil War and the bombing of Guernica heightening the official anxiety; the need to protect against gas attacks by the provision of gas masks and gas decontamination facilities; and the need to have available ready means of burying a large number of people in the event of heavy civilian casualties – a large number of cardboard coffins were produced as a stand-by.

Glyn Morgan recorded that,

the story, in chronological order, really commences as far back as 1935, when the Council in common with all other local authorities, was asked to consider in very broad outline their plans for defence against air attack, with the saving clause that such measures 'in no way imply a risk of war in the near future and they are wholly precautionary'. The initial 'Alert' on the 3rd September 1939 (which was actually a false alarm, as was that which sounded during the night of September 3rd to 4th) was followed by an 'Alert' about 7.30 a.m. on September 6th, during which an aeroplane passed over the town and a gun at the Whalebone battery fired three or four rounds. There was much excitement and speculation during the day, and the general opinion was that the aeroplane was, in fact, a British one.

124   *Advertisement for a privately issued indoor shelter. The council had issued sections of metal sheet enabling householders to construct a garden shelter in a pit which was then to be covered with earth, but these were not always popular as it took time to grab essentials while evacuating the house for the lesser comforts of the cramped temporary home.*

125   *The Fire Station at the bottom of Mawney Road engages volunteers for the process of building a sandbag wall for the protection of men and vehicles. Entertainment at the Plaza cinema and Romford Football Club had restarted after a temporary cessation following the outbreak of hostilities.*

126 *Rescue workers begin to dig out the ruins of a suburban house after a raid. For publication in the local newspapers an upbeat caption is attached: 'Proof of British quality – despite the fact that several tons of masonry fell on this small British-made car when a house was demolished recently, the only damage it sustained was a dented roof. As can be seen, not a pane of glass in the car was even cracked.' Identification of the street was not given during the war, the phrase 'In South East England recently …' being used instead. In this case, no mention is made of any occupants of the houses, whether killed or injured in the raid.*

Nevertheless, Romford felt, somewhat proudly, that it had had its baptism of fire!

In the next few months things were quiet. The emphasis was on the social effects of the war while the efficient local authority provided public shelters at various strategic points, such as the open space at the north-east end of the market. One story in the *Romford Times* said that 'The remarkable allegation that the coach-travelling public of Romford, Hornchurch and Dagenham had been "hoodwinked" by the entire suspension of Green Line coach services to

London and that the Transport Board had used the national emergency as an excuse to withdraw the services completely was made at a meeting held at the *Bull Hotel* on Monday evening.' Many people relied on this express service to travel to work in Ilford, Stratford and London, rather than use the shabby, unreliable and overcrowded trains. A later report, on 29 November, announced that some of the Green Line coaches were being released from ambulance service and were likely to be restored to one of the local routes (the Y2 route). Another story, on 20 September, may have been a

127   *Two of the simpler wartime adverts used in local newspapers.*

morale booster. The headline read 'Romford is now a No.1 A.R.P. Town', the report noting 'Air Raid Precautions and Civil Defence measures in Romford are in such a complete and advanced state that the Council has won the confidence of the County Council and higher authorities to such an extent that the Borough is regarded as an example to others … Councils are turning their attention to detail, perfecting the schemes where the hurried plans of a week or two ago left any room for improvement.' It was felt that Alderman Forge, who had been directing ARP in Romford to such a high standard, should be re-elected Mayor.

Two other stories in local papers pointed out areas of hidden poverty caused partly by the war and the call-up of men who were the main providers, and often the only source of income, in a household. If the newly recruited soldier avoided his responsibility of providing money for essentials, women without the wherewithal for rent could actually be made homeless. On 29 November 1939 a headline ran 'Homeless girls scandal – roaming the local streets

– penniless, destitute; a war problem.' The report continued, 'An alarming number of girls who have lost their jobs through the war have been left penniless and homeless – without friends to assist them, they have wandered about. Many have been sleeping out, grateful for the most meagre shelter that chance may provide.' At this time certain words were not used in public and the journalist has been very careful with his headline.

A second story made an appeal for funds on 17 December 1937 under the headline 'How Romford's poor will spend Christmas', and quoted the Romford Social Service Association, one of the voluntary organisations set up by the Rotary Club and others in the difficult inter-war years, as saying, 'there are scores of cases of very real distress, including pensioners and children who have really inadequate footwear and heating to tide them over the very cold weather'.

Civil Defence preparations kept moving ahead. By the time the Battle of France, ending with the Dunkirk evacuation, was over,

MARCH 16th—22nd
ROMFORD'S
WAR WEAPONS
WEEK

GET READY TO MAKE YOUR MONEY FIGHT

Our War Weapons Week is coming! It will be our special chance to
help pay for the huge armaments needed to win this war. Let us
be ready—firms and individuals—to lend our savings to the nation.

INVEST ALL
YOU CAN IN

3% SAVINGS BONDS
2½% NATIONAL WAR BONDS
3% DEFENCE BONDS
SAVINGS CERTIFICATES
and
POST OFFICE SAVINGS BANK

Double your Group Subscription. Start a
new Group in your factory, office or street.
Hit back at Hitler. Hit harder than ever
in War Weapons Week.

WHERE TO BUY	
SAVINGS BONDS and WAR BONDS	Bank Stockbroker Post Office
DEFENCE BONDS	Post Office Bank Stockbroker
SAVINGS CERTIFICATES	Post Office Bank Savings Group

MAKE OUR WAR WEAPONS WEEK A TRIUMPH

128 *Romford's War Weapons Week was one of several campaigns for savings. Warship Week raised an amazing £420,000 to construct HMS Raider.*

some 6,763 persons could be seated in street shelters. Later on, bunks were introduced when it was realised that sheltering from raids could be a long job. This reduced accommodation so now there was sleeping space for 2,589. Everyone was busily putting the final touches to their 'Anderson' shelter in the garden, as by August 1940 it seemed that the enemy would definitely launch large-scale air attacks. Some shelters were adapted to incorporate the individual's ideas of comfort after locals realised they would need to spend more than an hour or two at

a time in shelters – alerts could be short or long, and several could occur over the course of a day or night, and all-night sessions could even be expected. As Glyn Richards wrote, 'Many pet gadgets had to give place to bunk-room and much ingenuity had to be expended in converting a shelter which easily accommodated six persons sitting … into a bedroom which, with great difficulty, housed the same number lying down.' The 'Anderson' garden shelter was really very limited for space, and many people adopted alternative routines as the blitz continued from 7 September 1940 until May 1941. In Romford there were no deep shelters, like the Underground railway stations in London, so some sheltered in another government idea, the Morrison shelter, a steel-framed box with wire mesh sides that could be fitted under a large dining table and enabled people to stay in the house. Others ignored raids at home and slept in their normal beds, chancing the risk of a bomb hitting the building. Workplaces often had their own shelters in specially strengthened cellars; a government pamphlet gave instructions for the strengthening process.

Romford people had become accustomed to living in wartime. In the rescue and Civil Defence services, many women necessarily took on what had been men's jobs, as others had done in the munitions factories in the First World War. Teenagers too young to join up had a role delivering messages and acting as despatch riders. Wardens who manned local ARP posts, reporting incidents and forming a link in each neighbourhood with other units, were often older men working in shifts before and after the day job, and some women served as wardens too. Special credit has to be given to the tough women drivers who kept Civil Defence transport moving, sometimes when the town was under attack. Anyone who spent too long

129 *An incident that aroused both local and national interest occurred on 21 September 1940 between Stanley Avenue and Carlton Road, Romford, when a parachute mine crashed into the ground causing a huge crater to appear in the back gardens. It was said to be the largest bomb crater in Essex during the war. The explosion demolished 20 homes and caused damage to more than 100 others. In a typical attempt to look on the bright side, it was said that the mine would have caused more damage and claimed more victims if it had exploded above ground rather than sinking deep down before it went off. This is the scene at the spot shortly after daylight.*

in the open during an air raid risked being killed or injured by shrapnel, pieces of shell, etc., often coming from friendly fire such as the gun site at Chadwell Heath, the local element in the ring of defensive guns barring the way to enemy bombers advancing up the Thames.

The government really developed its information and public relations service during the war. Even if there were sometimes unintended results in the posters, leaflets and broadcasts, it learned to use humour as a way of getting the message across. Keeping the population informed played a large part in its winning the war. However cynical people became, the government publications became increasingly popular in style when compared with the pre-war blue books and statistical compendiums, and made it look as though somebody at least knew how to win the war. Such initiatives accorded well with Winston Churchill's verbal dexterity in his messages to the public. The local papers regularly carried their quota of government adverts, giving advice in areas such as how to eke out meagre rations, save on fuel (most people had coal fires) and avoid waste.

Although not suffering the massive conflagrations that broke out over whole districts in the East End, particularly the Docklands area, Romford suffered a great deal of damage and many deaths and casualties during the blitz, and there was to be a second wave during 1944-5 when Hitler's vengeance weapons, the V1 doodlebug and V2 rocket, crashed down on the town in significant numbers. In between the blitz and the later horrors, repair work was sometimes done in a temporary fashion to keep life bearable.

Although they did not have proper weapons very often, the Home Defence recruits, first called the Local Defence Volunteers and, later, the Home Guard, consisted of men too old for the war and teenagers, who could themselves be a danger

130 *This rather strange photograph shows Borough Engineer F.V. Appleby conferring with local master builders as they survey the damage and work out the best way to carry out emergency repairs. Not seen here, in the less damaged section, are the many householders blasted out of their homes, their salvaged belongings stacked around them. A barrier with an oil lamp has been put across the road to prevent access. All emergency repairs were completed within eight days of the incident.*

131 *This garden shelter of brick, roofed with a slab of concrete, survives today in a Romford garden and belonged to an air-raid warden. It sounds as though Mr and Mrs Bishop were killed in this type of shelter, rather than the typical Anderson sunk into a pit and covered with earth.*

to local civilians. One incident in June 1940 involved local members of the LDV firing on civilian vehicles which failed to halt at road block checkpoints. The result of this was that four people were injured and a fifth was killed. At another incident in early June, two men from Bethnal Green who failed to stop their car at another checkpoint in Romford were fired upon.

Through personal memories we get glimpses of local life in wartime. A number of residents remember that during the blitz on east London people stood on the slightly higher ground in Mashiters Walk where they could see great fires raging in Docklands. In the logbook of London Road School for 4 September 1939 it was noted, 'School closed and to remain closed until further notice – owing to the outbreak of war.' A number of schools vacated the school building for purposes other than administration and drew up a rota for classes in teachers' homes, usually made up of children from the immediate area.

Some delays occurred in getting children evacuated to safer parts of England, often East Anglia. Children from Straight Road School were supposed to be taken to the railway station by buses from Barking Garage, but at the last moment a message came through that 'the garage has been bombed'. A message was transmitted to police at Gallows Corner, who booked lorry drivers and other vehicles to help take the children to the railway station. In another part of town, children to be evacuated from Mawney Road School were lining up in the playground for the checking procedure when the siren sounded for an air-raid warning. Evacuation had to be delayed while children were sent down to shelters beneath the playground until the raid was over. A sad incident occurred close to Romford in Globe Road, when an anti-aircraft shell landed on a back garden and a couple of pensioners were killed after their shelter collapsed and they were trapped beneath slabs of concrete. This was particularly poignant as Mr George Bishop and his wife had both been in the habit of taking refuge at night in the shelter, while many others stayed in their houses and yet escaped harm.

The arrival of VE Day brought people out into the streets and parks to celebrate. Many younger people travelled up to London where the parties were bigger. British

132 *This photograph of Romford Market in the 1950s shows people wearing heavy, drab clothing, often mended and patched. Everybody soldiered on, hoping for better times.*

KILLWICK'S
HAVE ALL THE NEW DESIGNS   EST. 1850
SELECTED UTILITY FURNITURE
THE UTILITY BEDROOM SUITE WITH A NEW LOOK

4ft. FIGURED OAK BEDROOM SUITE comprising Double Door Wardrobe, Sunk Centre Dressing Table with 3 large bevelled mirrors and a fitted Tall Boy.

57 Gns. or **35/-** monthly.

STATION PARADE
5, 6, 7, 8, 9,
ROMFORD
Phone 1863   Phone 1863

133 *Killwick's of Station Parade, Romford are still selling 'utility' furniture, a feature of hard post-war times, constructed out of less solid materials than pre-war items were. These rather old fashioned pieces claimed to be 'New Look' but were similar to what had been in vogue for years.*

Our very latest design ——
the "IMPERIAL" SUITE
NOTE THE ROUNDED CORNERS ONLY SEEN ON
QUALITY FURNITURE

Figured Walnut BEDROOM SUITE
comprising: 4ft. Ladies' Wardrobe, Dressing
Table with large Cheval Mirror and large
fitted Gents' Robe, Mahogany lined through-
out including backs of Suite.   **£66.8.6**

4ft. Figured Walnut BEDSTEADS   **£8.2.4**
to match, and Spiral Spring.   Each

COLLYER & SONS
The Furnishing Specialists
SOUTH ST., ROMFORD
Near Ritz Cinema   Telephone: ROMFORD 0436   Next to Romford Station
'Buses Nos. 86a, 87, 103, 252, 370 stop outside the door

134 *An advert for Collyer's furniture business
has an illustration of the store which stood above
Regarth Avenue near the station. The site is now
used for housing. The word 'utility' had been
dropped by 14 July 1948, and, although not
mentioned, furniture rationing had ended.*

soldiers filtered back slowly from abroad.
Demobilisation went smoothly, unlike the
situation at the end of the First World
War. A simple priority formula had been
devised: two months' war service equalled
one year of age, so a serviceman of 22 with
four years' service had priority equal to a
man of 40 with one year's service. It was
planned that within a year three million
men and women would be demobbed. The
only problems were shortage of space in
ships and other transport, many of which
had been damaged, and lack of fuel. Service
people returning to the area discovered they
had often been better off in the services;
this was known as the 'price of peace'.
While everybody in Romford was happy
that the war was over and the dark shadow
of aerial bombardment was lifted, they
soon realised that Britain was battling to
make ends meet. Nearly all consumer items
were in short supply – clothing, food, beer,
cigarettes, petrol, cosmetics and houses.
Many factories had been turned over to war
production, there was a worldwide shortage
of materials, and Britain had bankrupted
itself fighting the war. The standard of living
was not high.

Before the war, many of the items we
take for granted today were non-existent
in the cost-conscious homes of ordinary
local citizens. Their houses were rarely
redecorated inside and thousands lacked
basic amenities. Families and individuals
rarely ate out, the exception being the
perennial fish and chips or faggots – truly
economic meals. Many thousands could not
even afford this treat regularly. By the end
of the war, however, some returnees and
civilians had nest-eggs, having been unable
to spend much of their income in wartime
conditions. There also appeared, as always
in times of shortage, black marketeers who
could obtain almost anything for a price.
After all, rationing in Britain was still in
force for many items and continued so until
about 1954.

Soldiers being discharged early for
medical reasons often found themselves
accosted with offers in the region of £20
(worth about £200 in today's money) for
their 'demob outfits', one real benefit
provided by the Forces and valued at £12.
It included a suit, a raincoat, a felt hat, a
shirt, two collars, two pairs of socks, a

135   *Silcock's Radio make the case for watching the London Olympics on TV.*

pair of shoes and a toilet kit. The racketeer would make a killing on this, the eager buyer relishing the additional opportunity of saving his allocation of 56 clothing coupons, themselves a hot currency. Some local people wanted to improve the look of their homes but little could be done in the way of work as the building trade was tied up repairing war damage to every kind of building that had suffered problems in the war. Towards the end of the conflict adverts had appeared in newspapers looking forward to the possibility of a return to normal supplies of all products. Ford put out an advert headed 'Until Then'. 'When gay paints are made again, faded furniture will become bright, and husbands and wives will pleasantly wrangle over the colour of

their new Ford cars. Until Then, "Make do and Mend" as our slogan, the unique Ford Service Facilities will ensure the efficient and economical running of thousands of Ford cars on work of National importance.' Romfordians and others were to wait a long time for the promised day.

In spite of the shortage of everything, there were several years during which pre-war interests were rekindled. The cinemas were madly popular, and in American films you glimpsed the more luxurious lifestyle that people had dreamed of during the dark days of the war. Sport was back in a big way, record attendances being recorded for motor-cycle speedway, greyhound racing, cricket and football. The glamour and excitement of these events were popular because they contrasted with most people's living conditions. Although the Romford area had seen a very large number of houses built in its suburbs in the 1930s, a large proportion of locals still lived in unimproved properties dating back to the 1900s and before. Domestic appliances were rare. Better-off residents sometimes owned a vacuum cleaner, a pre-war console TV with a tiny screen, an electric cooker and kettle and electric lighting. Many still had gas lighting. But few homes had central heating, and in most of those that did the system needed a solid-fuel boiler that took up a large amount of room, and circulated hot water through large-circumference pipes that would not have looked out of place in a factory. Cinema-goers goggled at opulent American homes, with refrigerators, washing machines, dishwashers, food mixers, and brightly coloured furnishings, curtains, carpets and paint. Californians had patios, loungers, barbecues and the joys of outdoor relaxation, whereas the average Romfordian returned home from the Rex, the Gaumont, the Odeon or the Vogue cinema to his own, usually rather damp residence. This might have a scullery rather than a kitchen, a gas- or oil-fired boiler to wash clothes, and a meat-safe (cupboard with slatted wire sides to aid ventilation, to keep the food in) rather than a fridge.

In the late 1940s, several events began to accelerate the pace of change and promised an enhanced lifestyle. The Olympic Games of 1948 were held in London and some controls on rationing were lifted. Local car dealers offered fresh models such as 'The magnificent new Hillman Minx! With synchromatic finger-tip gear change and a wealth of new features'. An official notice to all tea retailers stated, 'Once again you may re-nominate your tea suppliers if you wish. This will enable you to get more of the brand of tea your customers prefer.' Easy terms were now available from Fishers of 209-11 North Street (near the Parkside) on televisions, radiograms, radio sets, record players and portable gramophones. Townspeople now had the first opportunity since the war to consider buying the rather expensive option of a television set.

IX

NEW PROSPERITY

The news that a large estate was to be built over the rural fields to the north-west of Romford came as a considerable shock when it was revealed in the *Romford Times* of September 1945. The news broke before councillors were able to attend a special conference of the London County Council's Housing Committee disclosing details of the plan. The next week more information appeared in the Wednesday paper, revealing

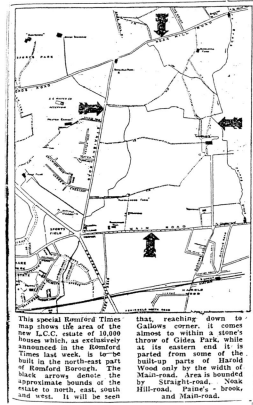

NO. 6331

WEDNESDAY, SEPTEMBER 26, 1945

Our 10,000 L.C.C. House Estate Plan Revelation Angers Romford Council

"A great dis-service to the public," "An abuse of privacy," and similar phrases, were used by members of Romford Council on Wednesday, when they criticized the exclusive story in last Wednesday's Romford Times revealing the plans of the L.C.C. for a 10,000 house estate—a "second Dagenham"—to be erected in the Straight-road—Noak Hill-road—Paines-brook—Main-road quadrangle. Our revelation caused a tremendous sensation throughout this area—particularly in the Gidea Park and Harold Wood areas.

The fierce denouncement was made, not because the story was inaccurate—there was no question of that—but on the mere fact that the Romford Times had published the story before the Council had been officially notified of the plan. The Council should, in their opinion, have been allowed to discuss the full proposal in private before informing the public of the intention.

Alderman C. E. Smart, who raised the matter, acknowledged that duty of the Press was to give news to the public, but he "deplored" fact that the story had appeared so soon. Four delegates, he said, had been appointed to interview chairman of Housing Committee of L.C.C., and were going the following day (Thursday). Matter had not been considered by the committee at all; it was, so far as Romford Council was concerned, completely in the privacy of L.C.C.

Only five people in the county were aware of it even, but the day before the conference they found the whole matter made public in the Press.

He did not criticize the Press; they had a job to do, but he felt very sorry about it. They were going on an errand which, unlike the Press, they knew very little about. Council had been asked to defer the matter, but

found, nevertheless, that full publicity had been given to it.

He was proud to belong to Romford Council, which had always carried on its business in the open and without secrecy, but there were occasions that demanded a certain amount of privacy This, apparently, had been abused, possibly by one of their members; however, he (Alderman Smart) now found himself in a position in which he would rather not go to the conference.

"PUBLIC DIS-SERVICE"

Alderman E. A. Forge said he agreed, and hoped the Mayor would take the same line, too. Alderman Forge was even more vehement in his condemnation of the story. He was considerably perturbed by the story, particularly as the Council had no official knowledge of the matter under discussion, yet it had appeared in the Press in full, as though it were a minute of the Council due for discussion.

"A great public dis-service has been done," he said, "in publishing this matter without consulting officials of this Council."

Mayor (Alderman A. J. Dyer) wound up the discussion by saying he also deprecated that sort of thing.

(See "Viewpoint," page 6.)

This special Romford Times map shows the area of the new L.C.C. estate of 10,000 houses which, as exclusively announced in the Romford Times last week, is to be built in the north-east part of Romford Borough. The black arrows denote the approximate bounds of the estate to north, east, south and west. It will be seen that, reaching down to Gallows corner, it comes almost to within a stone's throw of Gidea Park, while at its eastern end it is parted from some of the built-up parts of Harold Wood only by the width of Main-road. Area is bounded by Straight-road, Noak Hill-road, Paine's - brook, and Main-road.

136 *A new estate is planned, from the* Romford Times *of 26 September 1945.*

that more than 10,000 houses were planned. It was said that, prior to the 'leak', only five people in Essex were aware of the scheme. There had been no discussion by Romford Borough Council or consultation with local inhabitants. Councillors were soon using phrases such as 'A great disservice to the public', but this was mild compared with what the average citizen was saying. After more publicity was given to the excellent planning that was to be put into the scheme, the uproar quietened down.

A compulsory purchase order by the Ministry of Housing in 1948 paved the way for building to begin in earnest, and the first houses began to rise among the hills and fields. There were already a few scattered farmworkers' houses and other

country cottages in addition to an area of prefab houses along Straight Road. The first permanent estate house, 44 Gooshays Drive, was opened by the Chairman of the LCC, Walter R. Owen JP. It was semi-detached and contained five rooms, three of them bedrooms. The new residents, Mr and Mrs Rutherford, came from a five-roomed cottage at Becontree Heath, with three sons and four daughters. Mr Rutherford was a driver with the City Coach firm which had a garage at Brentwood. He had to be at his work at 4.50 in the morning, which involved getting up at 2.30a.m.

It was planned to build 7,600 permanent houses, a figure later amended to 8,566, 80 acres were to be set aside for factories north of the Colchester Road, 74 acres for

137 *Children enjoy an early Story Time in the library. Not a training shoe in sight, just Start-Rite sandals, kilts, a polka dot dress, cotton or Aertex shirts, short trousers with snake-belts, and home knitted woollies – a different world in 1961!*

138 *Romford Market in the 1950s, with a large number of cars passing through. Rumford Shopping Hall, as it was named, had not extended into the Victorian block on the right. The Pig in the Pound is still flourishing and the customers in the market on the whole look very prosperous.*

public parkland and 16.4 acres for shops. Thus employment in light industry would be available locally, and the work was designed to suit working mothers as well as the longer working week of men. The first arrivals at 'Little London', as it was nicknamed at first, found not a single bus service from the estate, and serious shopping involved a trek on foot or by bike to Romford.

The next few years saw the estate gradually acquire purpose-built schools, churches, shopping facilities, a library and a police station. Lord Morrison of Lambeth opened a new library on the estate in 1950,

pungently commenting that he was pleased to see the building 'looked as if it would not last too long'. He believed that the municipal buildings of his younger days were too long-lasting. For instance, the school he had attended in the 1890s was still standing: 'Not even Hitler could destroy it.' He explained that a new type of library might possibly be evolved in the future, and there would then be a need for a rebuilding. Economy dictated the construction of light structures that would later be replaced.

On 29 January 1960, the *Romford Recorder* published details of the planned

139 *A happy group of dignitaries and governors at Royal Liberty School during the Coronation Summer Fete, on 11 July 1953. Romford Borough's first lady mayor sits third from left in the front row. The community spirit which marked 1953 – Coronation Year – seems apparent in the attitude of the group, the Union Jack fixed to the surface air-raid shelter giving the point extra weight. Its modest size says something about the times. The shelters, some of which still exist, have been carefully adapted to today's uses.*

new Harold Hill Community Centre, costing £38,000. Two halls, spacious committee rooms, changing rooms and a sun lounge were designed. The old centre, 'an ancient farmhouse', was to be demolished. The building was expected to take 12 months to complete. By 1965 an 'ultra-modern' swimming pool was nearing completion next to the community centre on Gooshays Drive.

By the 1950s Romford was beginning to feel the pressures imposed by too many cars, as more and more people became motorists. The council was considering ways of improving the situation. Under the headline 'A start on Romford High Street at long last', a newspaper report of June 1956 read, 'After years of planning and agitating Romford Council will be told tonight by the Highways Committee that Minister of Transport Harold Watkinson is prepared to consider granting money this year on the Improvement of High Street, the widening of which will free a bottleneck which hampers the traffic stream from the London direction. The Minister has told the Committee that he will (also) consider approving a grant at an estimated cost of £23,000. Further improvement will be to the Upper Brentwood Road railway bridge – a £13,000 project.' At one stage there was a plan to knock down the *Golden Lion*, Romford's historic crossroads inn. The local council produced a public information film on the problems and the chairman of the relevant committee, Councillor Pat Ridley, was seen around the town pointing out the ways in which the road network might be improved. This led eventually to a scheme for a ring road to avoid the High Street and the Market altogether, the cost of which meant that it had to be carried out in sections. The first section, St Edward's Way, was ready in 1969, and an excited crowd attended the ceremony to close the Market.

The sad news of King George VI's death in 1952 ushered in a new Elizabethan era,

140 *South Street in the late '50s, the heyday of bus travel. This form of transport could move people quickly and efficiently from and to the town centre, and had much less far to travel before ring roads, roundabouts and one-way streets added to journey lengths. Notice the old signpost pointing to Chelmsford and London, and the very determined phalanx of ladies storming across the pedestrian crossing, the change of lights having halted the traffic. A selection of the 18 different London Transport bus and coach routes serving Romford is visible, plus the 2A Eastern National route to Southend.*

141 *A view along the River Rom, showing old buildings that have disappeared with the modernisation of Romford. The photograph is taken from the parapet of the old bridge over the High Street, built in the 1960s.*

and the Borough of Romford issued an official Souvenir Brochure and Programme of Events to celebrate the new age. Fittingly, the foreword would be penned by Lilian Irons, the first lady to be Romford's First Citizen: 'As Mayor of Romford for Coronation Year, I am glad to send some words of greeting to the people of Romford. I feel very honoured to be the first woman Mayor of the town, the more so that it falls to me ... during the Coronation of Queen Elizabeth II. There are many functions which are being arranged in Romford during the Coronation period, and the festivities will not be confined to Coronation Day.' She goes on to say that she hopes Romford people will take full advantage of the occasion. The previous year's mayor, Alderman G. Roberts, who presided over the Coronation Committee which organised the events, also sent a message thanking 'those ladies and gentlemen who have given us their assistance and advice in various ways. I also want to thank the Organisations who have come

142 *This unusual house, slightly further along the River Rom in Como Street, shows another bit of character lost from the centre of Romford replaced by a modern housing development extending back along the street.*

143 *The former* Woolpack *pub, under threat at the time of writing. Most recently home to Secrets night club, not so long ago the building carried a plaque with the information that Edward Ind of the brewery family had lived there in the 19th century. The High Street was very narrow at this point and the constriction prevented the town from voting 'Yes' to tramways at the beginning of the 20th century.*

144 *The erstwhile Wedding Gallery building at 37-9 North Street was regarded as making a positive contribution in the 2000 Heritage Strategy of the Borough. The building is late 18th-century, and not seen in the photograph is the hipped mansard roof with weatherboarded sides at the top. There is also a centrally placed winder staircase. In spite of English Heritage pointing out many interesting features and assessing that 'this late C18 building makes a positive contribution to the area for the elements of its form (as seen in the symmetrical front, the arrangement of the former sash windows and the old tiled roof) that suggest its early date', the advisers gave no encouragement for its retention or listing. Romford cries out for a planning and conservation framework that would enable such buildings to be restored and rented out for suitable use so that future generations can appreciate the remaining heritage.*

forward with arrangements for organizing Coronation events.'

A permanent reminder and commemoration of the year was the restoration of the old burial ground next to the Town Hall in Main Road as a Coronation Garden. What had become neglected and overgrown was to have 'seats and flowers for the enjoyment of all, and there will be a special feature of sweet-smelling shrubs and plants for the enjoyment of blind persons'. The old Cemetery Chapel was transformed into a rose garden. It was only much later that the War Memorial was removed to this area. The main events in the brochure lasted from Saturday 30 May, beginning with Romford Carnival, until Sunday 14 June, when there was the start of a 120-mile road cycle race from the Market Place, organised by Dixie Wheelers Cycling Club, over a 19.5-mile circuit, passing through Havering to finish at Havering Green. The other final event on that day was a match between Romford and Hornchurch cricket clubs at the Brewery Sports Ground, Waterloo Road. There was also a long list of celebrations in schools open to the public, and the Town Hall was 'floodlit and decorated with coloured lights and bunting, and a portrait of the Queen will be displayed'.

Modern Romford:
A Final Word

Romford today is part of the London Borough of Havering but, looking into the future, it needs to consider other options. There have been advantages in belonging to London, but perhaps the area could have moved into the 'City' league as a separate entity. The London connection has brought with it an incessant seeking after growth and the pouring of concrete in an effort to rival Lakeside and Croydon. Those responsible for the planning process should value the character given to the town by interesting buildings which could be restored to an original state. Romford needs cultural depth. Similar towns in England boast small studio theatres and repertory cinemas, art galleries and museums. Romford is one of the most historic areas in the country but the powers that be seem determined to bury its history under a tide of development. The citizens would appreciate a 'greening' of the town centre, a great opportunity to restore some country charm to the town having been lost when the Brewery Centre was built. The

145 *This small bridge over the Rom, off St Edward's Way, shows how modern developers can show imagination and respect for the dignity of the urban landscape.*

146 *This scene inside the former Liberty Two also contributes imaginative elements to an everyday modern structure. The escalators seem to rise majestically within the impressively high atrium space.*

147 *This relic of Ind Coope's former brewery stands at the entrance to the modern Brewery Shopping Precinct. The sudden closing of the Romford Brewery Company, an efficient unit which had seen considerable sums spent on modernisation, shows what can happen when multinational companies call the local tune.*

new Oldchurch Hospital has been developed over a large part of a former parkland area. No equivalent area of park or playing field has been given back to the town on this location.

In summer 2006, Romford was celebrated on the stage of the National Theatre in a play entitled *Market Boy*, by local playwright David Eldridge. He had worked on the market in the 1980s in the era of Margaret Thatcher and understood that history was being made. It shows a recent chapter in the vibrant story of an institution which is over 750 years old. The play, brilliantly staged and performed, proved that others could see Romford's potential. Too many people from outside the town make vital decisions on behalf of the people who live here. Romfordians need to claim back their birthright. The first step is to stop building unnecessarily tall buildings and destroying those created by craftsmen in the past. Above all, councillors and officers, give us the museum for which we have the building, funds and enthusiastic committee and volunteers, but which has been blocked for so long.

BIBLIOGRAPHY

Evans, B.D., *Bygone Romford*, 1988

Evans, B.D., *Romford, Collier Row and Gidea Park*, 1994

Kelly's Directory of Essex from 1866-1937

Palmer, Susan J., 'Revolution or Evolution; the Rise of Retailing in Romford, 1919-1939' (thesis, 1987)

Richards, Glyn, *Ordeal in Romford* (Second World War), 1945

Romford Record (Journal of the Romford and District Historical Society), Nos 1 (1968) – 40 (2005)

Sparkes, I.G., *Gidea Hall and Gidea Park*, 1966

Terry, George, *Memories of Old Romford*, 1880

Victoria County History of Essex, Volume 7, 1978

Watt, Peter, *Hitler versus Havering*, 1994

INDEX

air-raid shelters, 92-3, 96, 104
Artists' Rifles, 65-70
As (Roman coin), 6

ballad, 'blind beggar of Bethnal Green',
    14
Banyard, Richard, 75
Barclays Bank, 77
Barking Abbey, 10
Benyon family, 33
    Richard, 39
Bibbings, Theresa, 57
Bigod, Roger, Earl of Norfolk, 11
Bray, Mr (chemist), 57
Brenor, Peter de, 14
Brewery Centre, 109
Brock's blouse factory, 67
bus services, 71, 83-8, 91, 105
Bush Elms, 12

car ownership, 62-3, 64, 71, 104-5
carriers, 30, 31, 43-4, 45
Cass, Christopher, 33
Caunt, George, 7
Caux, Harry de, 6
Chanelse Bridge, 10
charity school, 31
Charles I, King, 15, 25-6
Charlotte, Princess of Mecklenburgh-
    Strelitz, 36, 37
cinemas, 62, 70, 100
Cock and Bell Inn, 35
Collett's, T.F., 75
Collier Row, 11
Congregational Church, 78-9
Cooke: Ann, 25; Sir Anthony, 16, 20, 25;
    Sir Thomas, 79
Coronation:
    Committee, 106
    Garden, 108

Cotton, Nicholas, xi
Cottons Park, xi, 5
County Court, 47
Craddocks, 77
Crawland, John, xi
Crowlands, xi
'Crowlands' station, 83-8

Daldy and Co., 73
Delamare, Abraham, 39-40
demobilisation, 98
Dog Lane (Waterloo Road), xi, 45
Domesday Book, 9
Dover, Richard de, 13-14
Dovers Corner, 13
druids, 2
Durolitum, 2-3, 4-6

Edward the Confessor, 7-9
Edward VI, King, 20
Eldridge, David, 110
Elizabeth I, Queen, 20
Essex, Kingdom of, 7-8
Essex, Lord Lieutenant of, 31
Essex Chronicle, 36
Essex Militia, 31
evacuation, 96
Eyles, Sir John, 26, 30, 32-3, 34, 79

Factory Road (Terrace), 46-7
Fairfax, General, 27
fairs, 40, 41-3
Fawkes and White, 71, 73
First World War, 64-70
Fisk, Edward, 63-4
flooding, 55-7
Forge, Alderman, 92
Frostick and Sons, 75

Gallows Corner, 37-8

Gidea Hall, 16, 20, 22, 25-6, 30, 32-4, 33, 63, 68
Gidea Park, 4
    Garden Suburb, 32, 60-1, 63, 82
    Station, 45
Golden Lion, 47, 105
Goring, General, 26
Grafton, John Marmaduke, 38, 39-40
Great Essex Road, 10-11
    turnpiked, 30, 31, 34
Great Pettits, xi

Hammond, Bert, 2
handaxes, 1
Hare Hall camp, 66-7
Hare Hall Mansion, 40, 46, 65
Hare Street, 4, 5, 7, 30-1, 41, 65
Harold, King, 9
Harold Hill/Wood, 6
Harold Hill Estate, 101-4; Community Centre, 104
Havering chapel, 16-18
Havering halfpenny, 15
Havering Henge, 2
Havering-atte-Bower royal palace, 6-8, 11, 16-20, 80-2
Henry VIII, King, 19-20
Herde, John, 22
Hewitt, John, 64
highwaymen, 37-8
Hole, H.W., 75, 76
Holman (historian), 18-19
Home Guard, 95-6
Hornchurch, 10, 11, 15
Hoy, George, 49

Ind Coope, 59, 64, 77, 110. See also Romford Brewery
infirmary, 53, 70
insurance agents, 44
Ives, G., 75

John, King, 11
Johnson, Samuel (curate), 32

Kemp, Will, 21-4
Killwick's, 97

Lasham's, 58, 73, 85
Liberty of Havering, xi, 11, 15-19
Lea, river, 10
Library, 82, 102

Lodge Farm Estate, 82
London House, 23
Lowlands, 2
Lyson (historian), 19

Manny, Sir Walter de, xi
Marescall, xi
market, the, ii-iii, 29, 40, 41, 52, 53, 57, 72, 97, 103, 110
Marks, xi, 1, 15, 26-7
Marshall, xi, 1, 63, 70
Marshall Park School, xi
Masel, M., 73
Mashiter, Cuthbert, 39-40
Matilda (Maud), 10
Matthews, W.D., 53
Mawney Arms, 64
Mawneys, xi, 53
Mawneys Lane, xi
Meadmore's, 73
Medici, Marie de, 26
megalithic sites, 2, 5
Merk, Simon de, xi
Mildmay, Carew Hervey, 26-7
mills, 13-14, 46
Morant, 7, 19
Morgan, Glyn, 89-90
Morrison of Lambeth, Lord, 103
Mumford, Laurie, 54

New College, Oxford, 11-14
New Inn, 47
Noak Hill, 6
Norfolk Chronicle, 34
Norwich Post, 36

Ogborne, Elizabeth, 19
Oldchurch, xi, 10-11; Hospital, 110; Road, 49
Olympic Games, 1948, 100
Owen, Walter R., 102

Palmer, Isaac, 36, 40
Palmer, John, 34, 41
parade ground, 45
Park View Estate, 88
Petit, Thomas, xi
Pettits Lane, xi
Poel Brothers, 75
Poor Law, 39, 49
postal services, 34-6, 38, 40, 43
Prince Albert, 47

Priory of St Nicholas and St Bernard, Hornchurch, 10-11
Punch, 49
Pyrgo, 16, 20

Quarles, Francis, 24, 25
Quarter Sessions, 38
Queens House, 37

railway, 45-9, 55
Rainham, 6
Raphael, Herbert Henry, 63
Raphael Park, 32, 63
rationing, 98-9
Repton, Humphry, 39, 41, 42
Retreat, the, 21
Rise Park Estate, 82
Risebridge, xi
Rising Sun, 46
Roger Reede's charity, 49
Rom, river, 1, 4, 5, 7, 13, 55, 106, 109
Roman finds, 5-6
Roman road, 2-4, 7
Roman villa (Collier Row), 6
Romford: becomes a borough, 79; becomes a parish, 39; first appearance, 11
Romford Bowling Green Club, 31-2
Romford Brewery, 45, 55, 56-7
Romford Committee, 27-8
Romford Common, 6, 31
Romford Cricket Club, 51, 52, 54-5, 108
Romford Football Club, 51, 53-4
Romford Golf Club, 63
Romford Races, 31
Romford Times, 100, 101
Romford Union workhouse, 49-53
Rotary Club, 80, 92
Round House, the, 40
Rutherford, Mr and Mrs, 102

St Andrew's chapel, xi, 11
St Edward's Church, 21, 44
St Edward's Way, 105
Salmon (historian), 19
Saxons, 6, 8

Seabrook Estate, 83
Second World War, 82, 89-98
shops (and traders), 40, 63, 71, 82
Silcocks, 77, 99
smallpox, 36-7
Smarts, 77
Smith, Harold, 15-16
Smithfield, William, 36
Spivey, Diane, 27-8
Springham, Mr, 48
Squirrels Heath locomotive depot, 46, 47
stage-coaches, 30, 31, 38, 40, 44-5
station, 45, 47-8, 62
Stewards, 24; map, xi, 12, 25
Stickleback Bridge, 7
Stow, John, 10
Sun Inn, the, xi, 29
Swan, the, 24
swimming bath, 82, 104
Sydenham, Sir Edward, 25
Symonds, John, 16

tannery, 29
Thirlwell, F.H., 53
Tipper, Job, 40
Tolbutt, Edward, 45, 48
Town Hall, 86, 108
turnpikes, 32, 34

Ulmis, de (family), 12
Unicorn, the, 65
Upward, Dr Harold, 64
Urswick, xi; Thomas, 15

Wackett, W., 73
Wallenger, John Arnold, 40
Walthamstow, 1
war memorial, 69-70
Whalebone, 37-8
White Hart Hoppet, 63, 77
White Hart Hotel, 28, 53
William I, King, 9
Williamson's, 79
Woolpack Inn, 37, 107
Wright, Dr Alfred, 57, 78